College of the Ouachitas

A TREASURY OF XXth CENTURY MURDER

The Lives of
Sacco & Vanzetti

NBM
ComicsLit

A Special Treasury Edition was
made available only directly from
us strictly limited to 25 numbered
copies, bound in real cloth and
including an original plate signed
and numbered by Rick Geary,
with a silver-stamped jacket.

For more information:
800 886 1223, www.nbmpub.com.

ISBN: 978-1-56163-605-1
Junior Library Guild Edition: ISBN: 978-1-56163-622-8
Library of Congress Control Number: 2011927818
© 2011 Rick Geary
Printed in China

1ˢᵗ printing June 2011

Comicslit is an imprint
and trademark of

NANTIER · BEALL · MINOUSTCHINE
Publishing inc.
new york

THE LIVES OF
SACCO AND VANZETTI

♦
THE CRIME
♦
THE EVIDENCE
♦
A GLOBAL CAUSE

ANARCHISTS
&
IMMIGRANTS
!

VILLAINS
OR
VICTIMS
?

WRITTEN AND ILLUSTRATED BY
RICK GEARY

Also available by Geary:
A Treasury of Victorian Murder:
Vol. 1, pb.: $9.95
Jack The Ripper pb.: $9.95
The Borden Tragedy, pb.: $8.95
The Fatal Bullet, pb.: $9.95
The Mystery of Mary Rogers
hc.: $15.95
The Beast of Chicago pb.: $9.95
The Murder of Abraham Lincoln
pb.: $9.95, hc.: $15.95
The Case of Madeleine Smith
pb.: $8.95, hc.: $15.95
The Bloody Benders
pb.: $9.95, hc.: $15.95
A Treasury of XXth Century Murder:
The Lindbergh Child
pb.: $9.95, hc.: $15.95
Famous Players
pb.: $9.95, hc.: $15.95
The Axe-Man of New Orleans
hc.: $15.99

See more on these
at our website:
www.nbmpublishing.com

P&H: $4 1st item, $1 each addt'l.

We have over 200 titles,
write for our color catalog:
NBM
40 Exchange Pl., Suite 1308,
New York, NY 10005

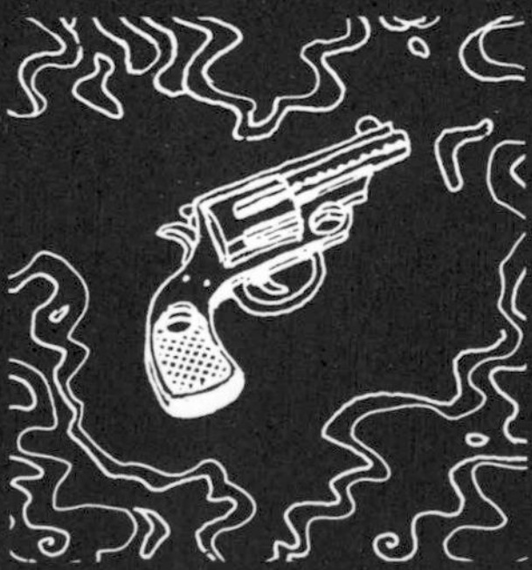

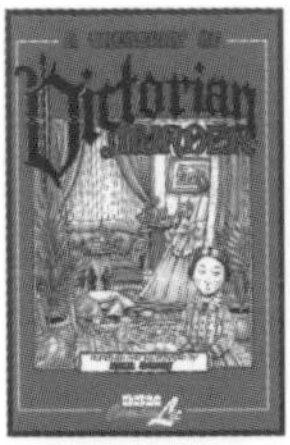
Victorian
Murder

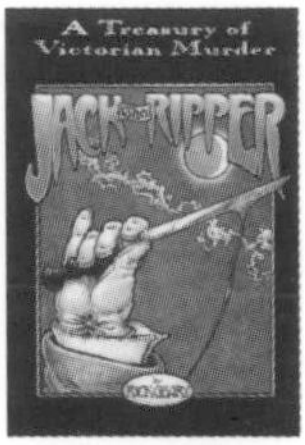
A Treasury of
Victorian Murder
Jack the Ripper

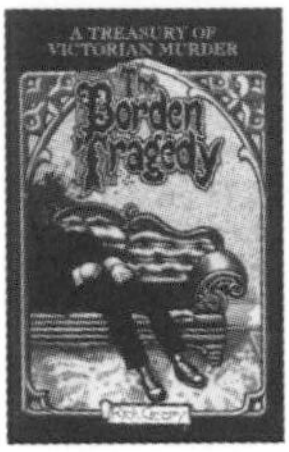
A TREASURY OF
VICTORIAN MURDER
The Borden Tragedy
RICK GEARY

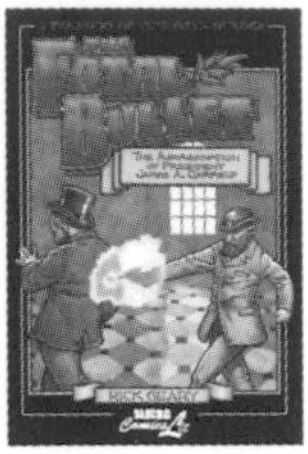
RICK GEARY

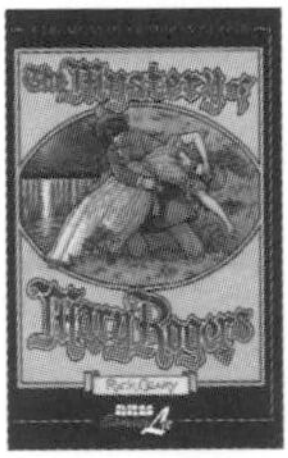
Mary Rogers
RICK GEARY

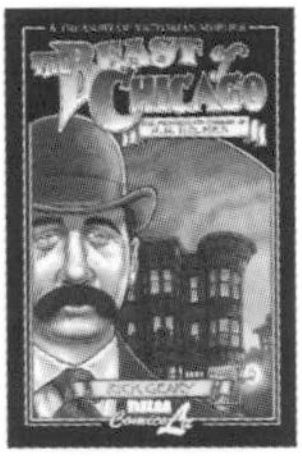
The Beast of Chicago
RICK GEARY

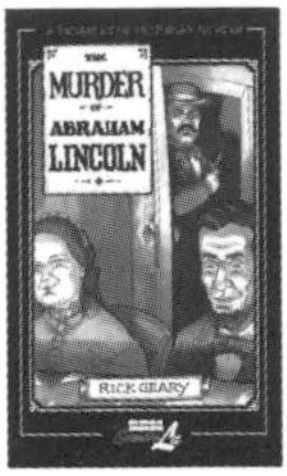
MURDER
ABRAHAM
LINCOLN
RICK GEARY

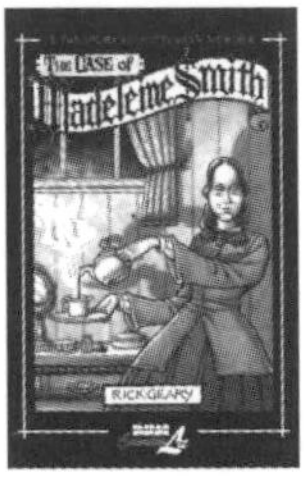
The Case of
Madeleine Smith
RICK GEARY

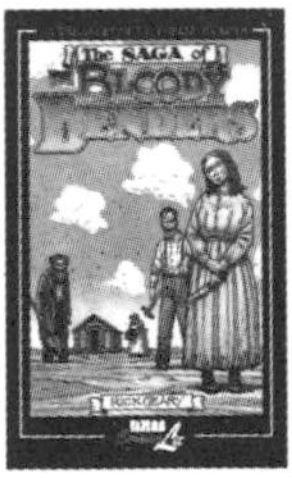
The SAGA of
RICK GEARY

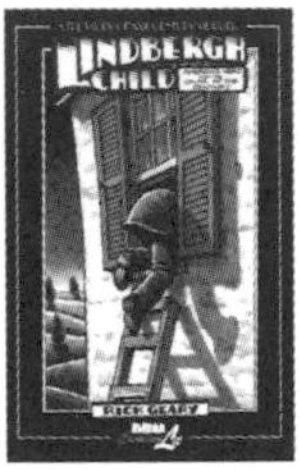
LINDBERGH
CHILD
RICK GEARY

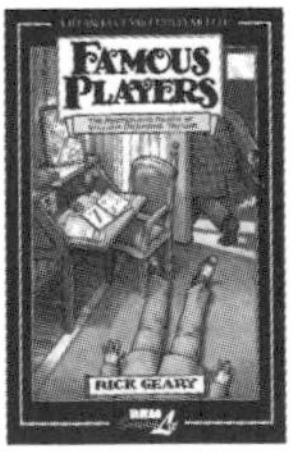
FAMOUS
PLAYERS
RICK GEARY

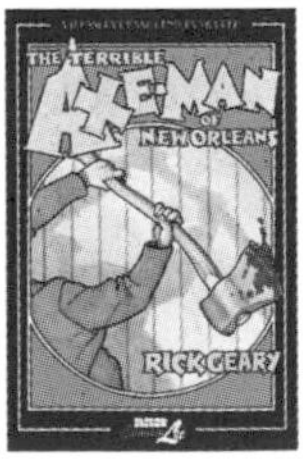
THE TERRIBLE
AXE-MAN
OF
NEW ORLEANS
RICK GEARY

THE LIVES OF SACCO & VANZETTI

BIBLIOGRAPHY

Blumenfield, Harold, *Sacco and Vanzetti, Murderers or Murdered?*
(New York, Scholastic Book Services, 1972)

Frankfurter, Marion Denham and Gardner Jackson, eds.,
The Letters of Sacco and Vanzetti. (Secaucus NJ, Citadel Press, 1956)

Joughlin, Louis and Edmund M. Morgan, *The Legacy of Sacco & Vanzetti.*
(Princeton NJ, Princeton University Press, 1976)

Mappen, Marc, *Murder and Spies, Lovers and Lies: Settling the Great Controversies of American History.* (New York, Avon Books, 1996)

Russell, Francis, *Tragedy in Dedham, The Story of the Sacco-Vanzetti Case.*
(New York, McGraw-Hill Book Company, 1971)

Temkin, Moshik, *The Sacco-Vanzetti Affair: America on Trial.*
(New Haven CT, Yale University Press, 2009)

Watson, Bruce, *Sacco & Vanzetti.* (New York, Penguin Books, 2007)

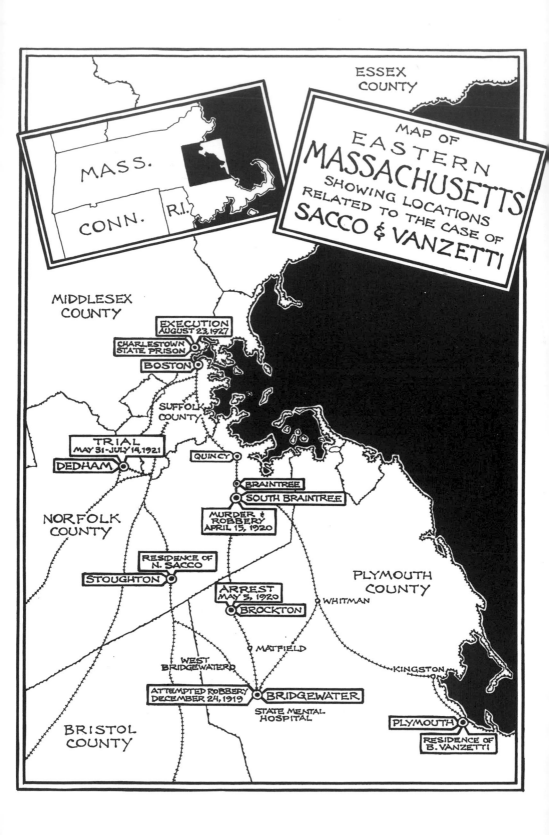

ESSEX
COUNTY

MASS.

CONN.   R.I.

MAP OF
EASTERN
MASSACHUSETTS
SHOWING LOCATIONS
RELATED TO THE CASE OF
SACCO & VANZETTI

MIDDLESEX
COUNTY

EXECUTION
AUGUST 23, 1927

CHARLESTOWN
STATE PRISON

BOSTON

SUFFOLK
COUNTY

TRIAL
MAY 31-JULY 14, 1921

DEDHAM

QUINCY

BRAINTREE

SOUTH BRAINTREE

MURDER &
ROBBERY
APRIL 15, 1920

NORFOLK
COUNTY

RESIDENCE OF
N. SACCO

STOUGHTON

ARREST
MAY 5, 1920

BROCKTON

WHITMAN

PLYMOUTH
COUNTY

MATFIELD

WEST
BRIDGEWATER

KINGSTON

ATTEMPTED ROBBERY
DECEMBER 24, 1919

BRIDGEWATER

STATE MENTAL
HOSPITAL

BRISTOL
COUNTY

PLYMOUTH

RESIDENCE OF
B. VANZETTI

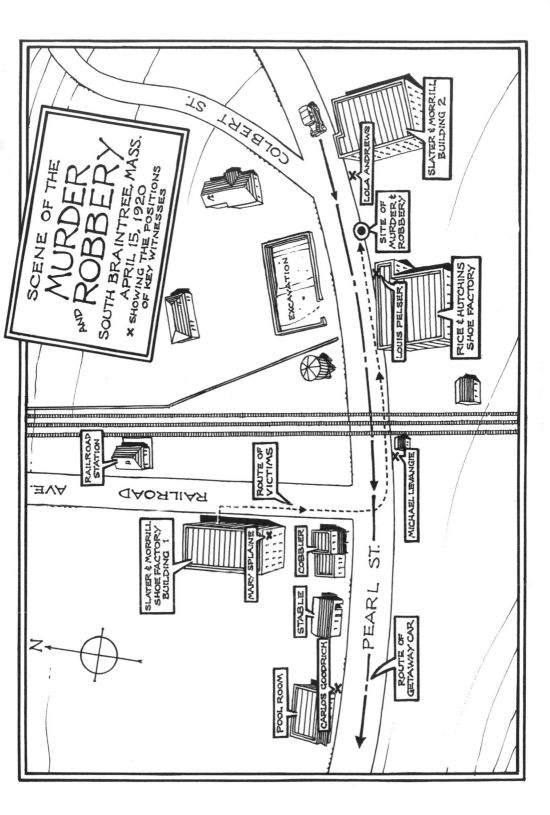

SCENE OF THE
MURDER
AND
ROBBERY
SOUTH BRAINTREE, MASS.
APRIL 15, 1920
× SHOWING THE POSITIONS
OF KEY WITNESSES

N

COLBERT ST.

EXCAVATION

SLATER & MORRILL
BUILDING 2

LOLA ANDREWS

SITE OF
MURDER &
ROBBERY

LOUIS PELSER

RICE & HUTCHINS
SHOE FACTORY

RAILROAD STATION

RAILROAD AVE.

ROUTE OF VICTIMS

MICHAEL LEVANGIE

SLATER & MORRILL
SHOE FACTORY
BUILDING 1

MARY SPLANE

COBBLER

STABLE

POOL ROOM

CARLOS GOODRICH

PEARL ST.

ROUTE OF GETAWAY CAR

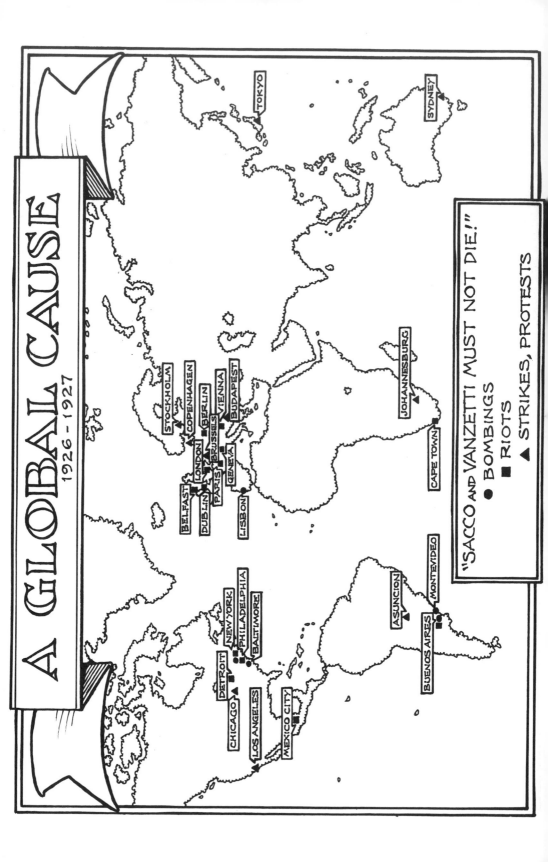

A GLOBAL CAUSE
1926 - 1927

"SACCO AND VANZETTI MUST NOT DIE!"

● BOMBINGS
■ RIOTS
▲ STRIKES, PROTESTS

TOKYO
SYDNEY
STOCKHOLM
COPENHAGEN
BERLIN
VIENNA
BUDAPEST
LONDON
BRUSSELS
PARIS
GENEVA
BELFAST
DUBLIN
LISBON
JOHANNESBURG
CAPE TOWN
NEW YORK
PHILADELPHIA
BALTIMORE
DETROIT
CHICAGO
LOS ANGELES
MEXICO CITY
ASUNCION
BUENOS AIRES
MONTEVIDEO

PART I

THE CRIME

THURSDAY, APRIL 15, 1920
SOUTH BRAINTREE, MASSACHUSETTS

THE DAY BEGINS MUCH LIKE ANY OTHER IN THIS QUIET
INDUSTRIAL TOWN TWELVE MILES SOUTH OF BOSTON.

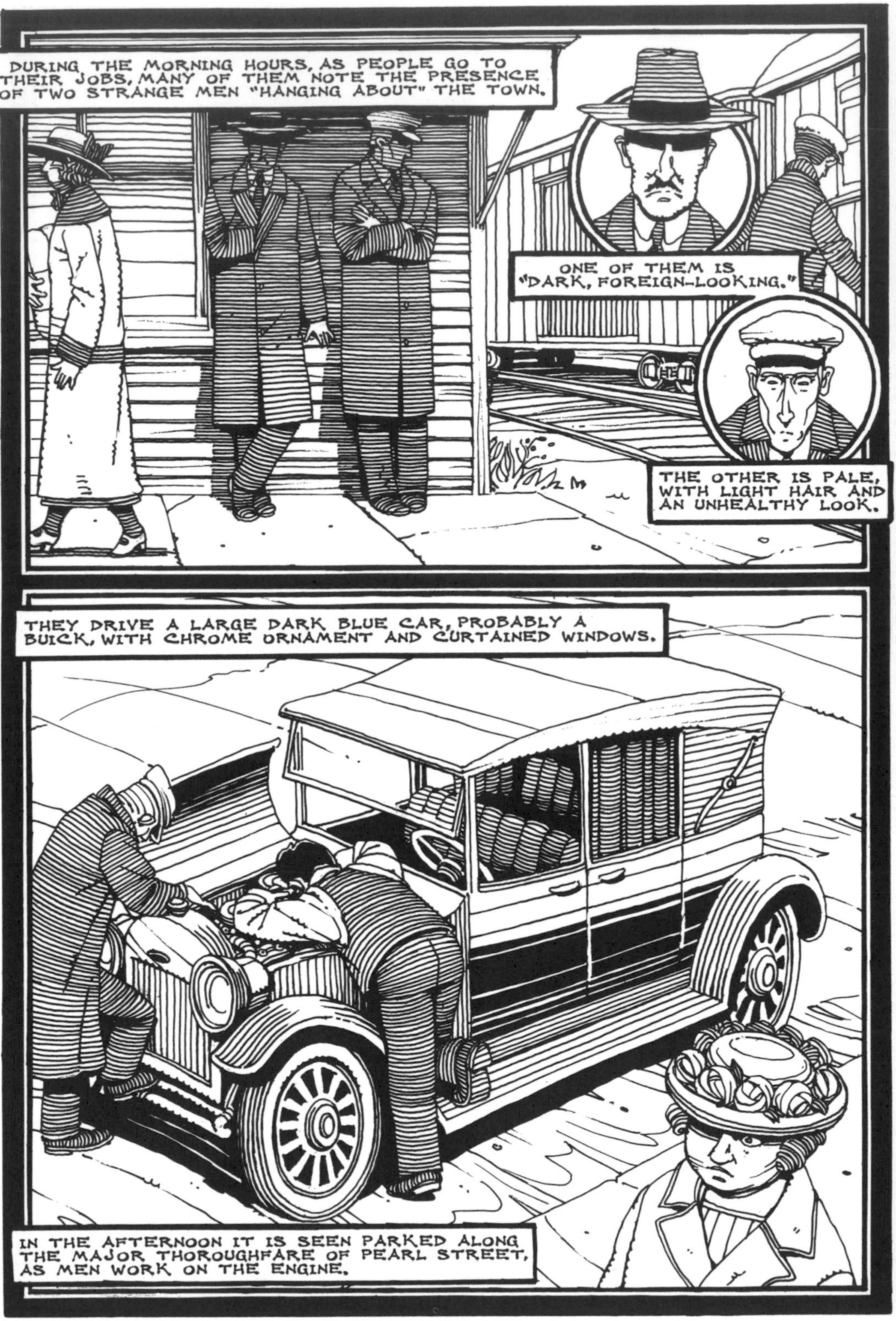
DURING THE MORNING HOURS, AS PEOPLE GO TO THEIR JOBS, MANY OF THEM NOTE THE PRESENCE OF TWO STRANGE MEN "HANGING ABOUT" THE TOWN.
ONE OF THEM IS "DARK, FOREIGN-LOOKING."
THE OTHER IS PALE, WITH LIGHT HAIR AND AN UNHEALTHY LOOK.
THEY DRIVE A LARGE DARK BLUE CAR, PROBABLY A BUICK, WITH CHROME ORNAMENT AND CURTAINED WINDOWS.
IN THE AFTERNOON IT IS SEEN PARKED ALONG THE MAJOR THOROUGHFARE OF PEARL STREET, AS MEN WORK ON THE ENGINE.

ONE OF THE LARGEST EMPLOYERS IN TOWN IS THE SLATER AND MORRILL SHOE FACTORY.

TODAY IS THE DAY WHEN PAY ENVELOPES ARE DISTRIBUTED.

DESPITE RECENT ROBBERIES IN THE AREA, THE PAYROLL IS DISBURSED IN CASH.

AT THE COMPANY'S BUILDING #1 THE ASSISTANT PAYMASTER, FREDERICK PARMENTER, AND A GUARD, ALESSANDRO BERARDELLI, COLLECT THE MONEY, WHICH HAS BEEN SORTED INTO 500 ENVELOPES.

THE ENVELOPES ARE STACKED INTO TWO WOODEN BOXES WHICH ARE PLACED INTO TWO STEEL CASES.

THEIR USUAL AUTO BEING UNAVAILABLE, THE MEN WALK WITH THE CASES...

WHICH CONTAIN A TOTAL OF $15,776. 51.

THEIR 200-YARD ROUTE TAKES THEM DOWN RAILROAD AVENUE, THEN LEFT UP PEARL STREET, PAST THE RICE & HUTCHINS SHOE FACTORY TO SLATER & MORRILL'S BUILDING #2.

PEARL ST.

RICE & HUTCHINS

SLATER MORRILL #2

CITIZENS ON THE SIDEWALK GREET THEM AS THEY PASS.

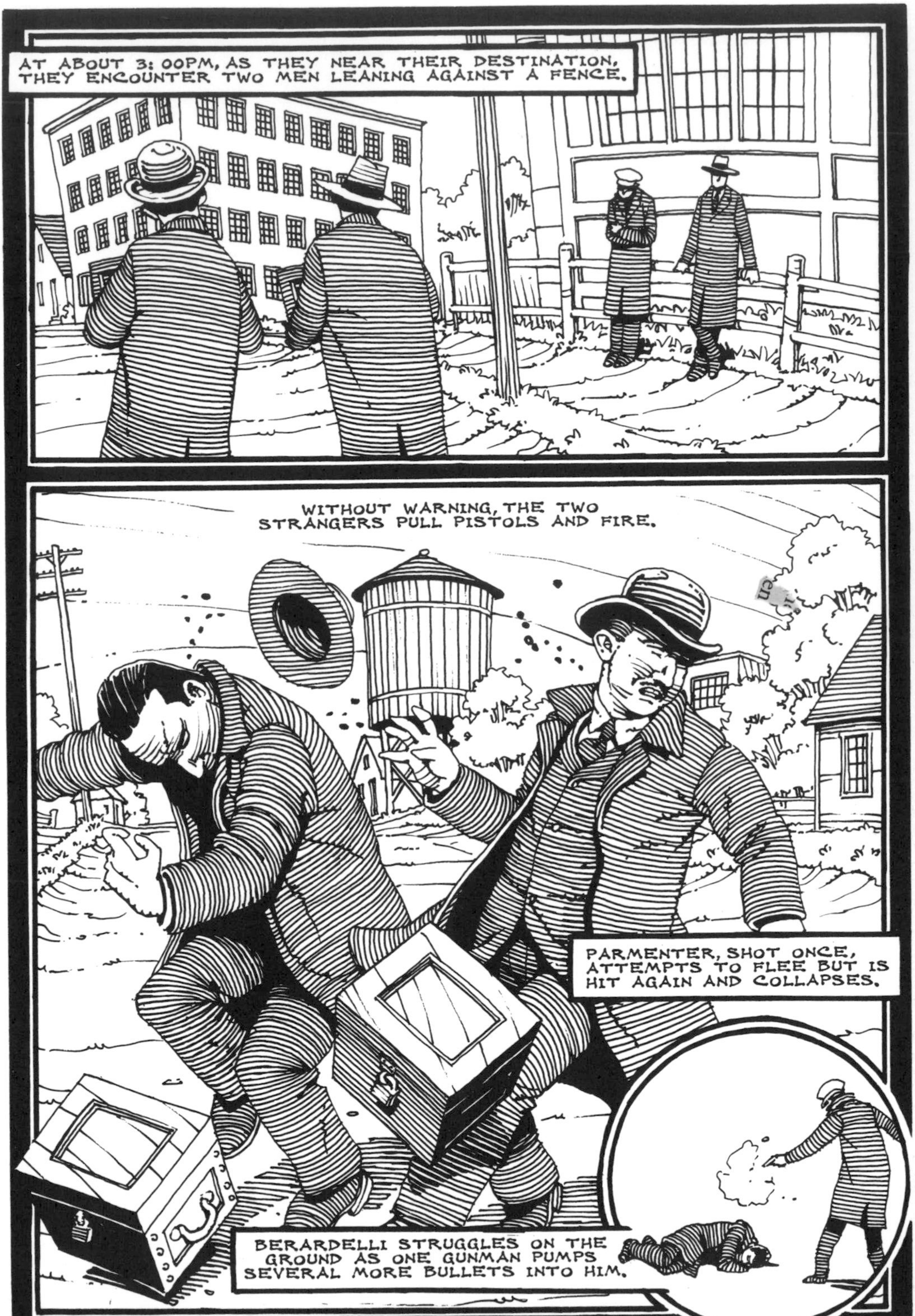
AT ABOUT 3:00PM, AS THEY NEAR THEIR DESTINATION, THEY ENCOUNTER TWO MEN LEANING AGAINST A FENCE.
WITHOUT WARNING, THE TWO STRANGERS PULL PISTOLS AND FIRE.
PARMENTER, SHOT ONCE, ATTEMPTS TO FLEE BUT IS HIT AGAIN AND COLLAPSES.
BERARDELLI STRUGGLES ON THE GROUND AS ONE GUNMAN PUMPS SEVERAL MORE BULLETS INTO HIM.

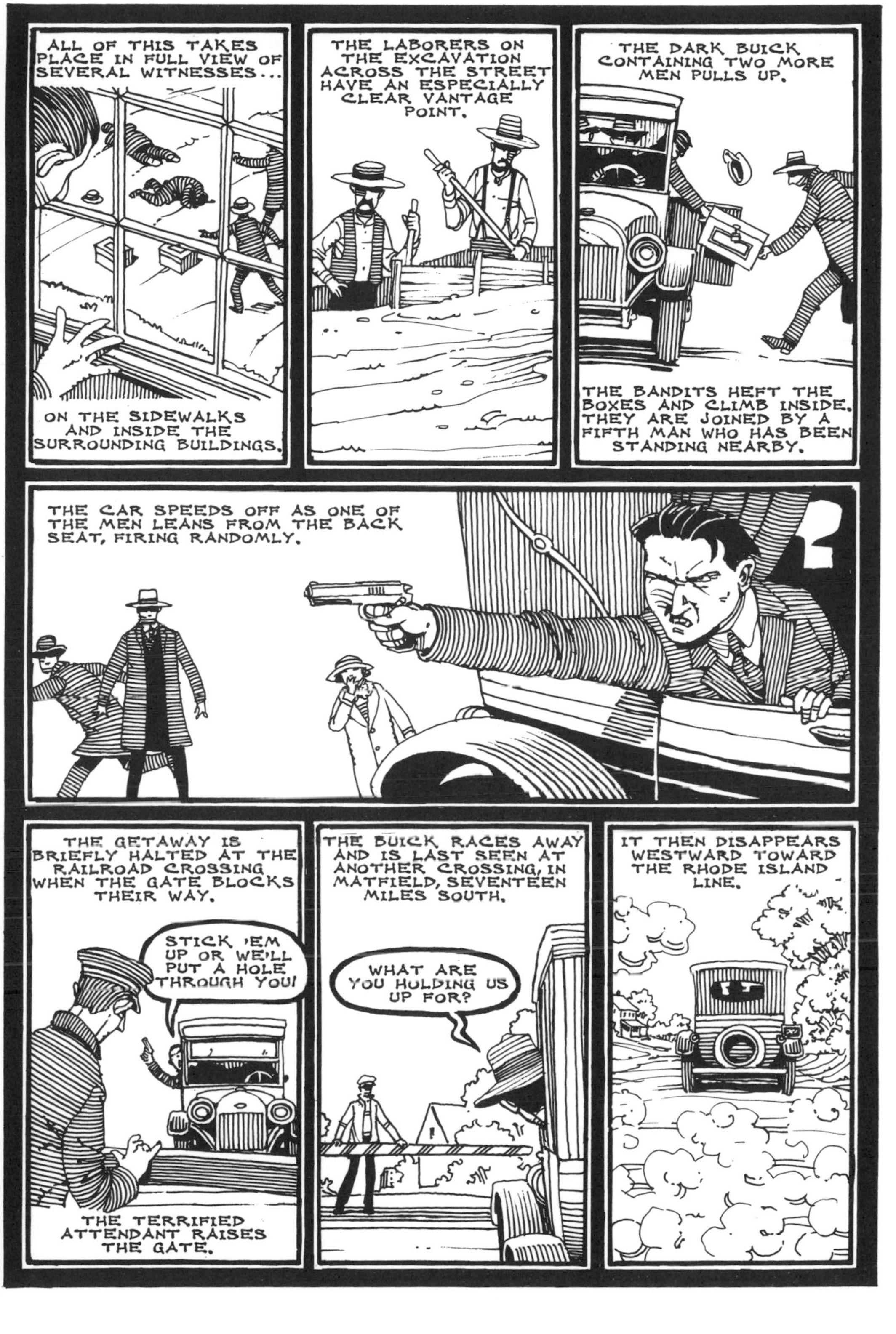
ALL OF THIS TAKES PLACE IN FULL VIEW OF SEVERAL WITNESSES...
ON THE SIDEWALKS AND INSIDE THE SURROUNDING BUILDINGS.
THE LABORERS ON THE EXCAVATION ACROSS THE STREET HAVE AN ESPECIALLY CLEAR VANTAGE POINT.
THE DARK BUICK CONTAINING TWO MORE MEN PULLS UP.
THE BANDITS HEFT THE BOXES AND CLIMB INSIDE. THEY ARE JOINED BY A FIFTH MAN WHO HAS BEEN STANDING NEARBY.
THE CAR SPEEDS OFF AS ONE OF THE MEN LEANS FROM THE BACK SEAT, FIRING RANDOMLY.
THE GETAWAY IS BRIEFLY HALTED AT THE RAILROAD CROSSING WHEN THE GATE BLOCKS THEIR WAY.
STICK 'EM UP OR WE'LL PUT A HOLE THROUGH YOU!
THE TERRIFIED ATTENDANT RAISES THE GATE.
THE BUICK RACES AWAY AND IS LAST SEEN AT ANOTHER CROSSING, IN MATFIELD, SEVENTEEN MILES SOUTH.
WHAT ARE YOU HOLDING US UP FOR?
IT THEN DISAPPEARS WESTWARD TOWARD THE RHODE ISLAND LINE.

BACK AT THE CRIME SCENE A LARGE CROWD GATHERS, AS POLICE ATTEMPT TO ROUND UP WITNESSES AND RECONSTRUCT EVENTS.

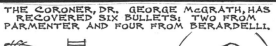

BERARDELLI IS DEAD AT THE SCENE. PARMENTER, TAKEN TO A HOSPITAL, DIES THE FOLLOWING DAY LEAVING A WIFE AND TWO SMALL CHILDREN.

SATURDAY, APRIL 17 AN INQUEST IS HELD IN THE TOWN OF QUINCY.

26 WITNESSES DESCRIBE THE BANDITS AND THEIR CAR. SINCE THE INCIDENT HAPPENED SO QUICKLY, FEW OF THEM CAN OFFER A PRECISE RECOLLECTION.

THE CORONER, DR. GEORGE McGRATH, HAS RECOVERED SIX BULLETS: TWO FROM PARMENTER AND FOUR FROM BERARDELLI.

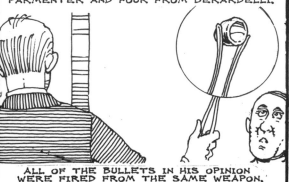

ALL OF THE BULLETS IN HIS OPINION WERE FIRED FROM THE SAME WEAPON.

THE CONSENSUS AMONG LAW OFFICERS IS THAT THIS CRIME WAS THE WORK OF PROFESSIONAL THIEVES.

BUT CHIEF MICHAEL STEWART OF THE BRIDGEWATER POLICE HAS OTHER IDEAS.

HE IS STILL INVESTIGATING AN ATTEMPTED ROBBERY IN HIS TOWN LAST CHRISTMAS EVE.

WEDNESDAY DECEMBER 24 1919: A PAYROLL TRUCK FOR THE L.Q. WHITE SHOE CO. WAS ATTACKED BY TWO ARMED MEN.

ONE OF THEM FIRED A SHOTGUN.

THE TRUCK SWERVED INTO A TELEPHONE POLE ATTRACTING SEVERAL ONLOOKERS.

AND THE WOULD-BE ROBBERS FLED IN A HUDSON AUTOMOBILE.

STEWART BELIEVES THAT THIS ATTEMPT WAS MADE BY A GANG OF ITALIAN "REDS" AND "BOLSHEVIKS"...

AND THERE IS A GOOD CHANCE THAT THE SOUTH BRAINTREE CRIME WAS THE WORK OF THE SAME GROUP.

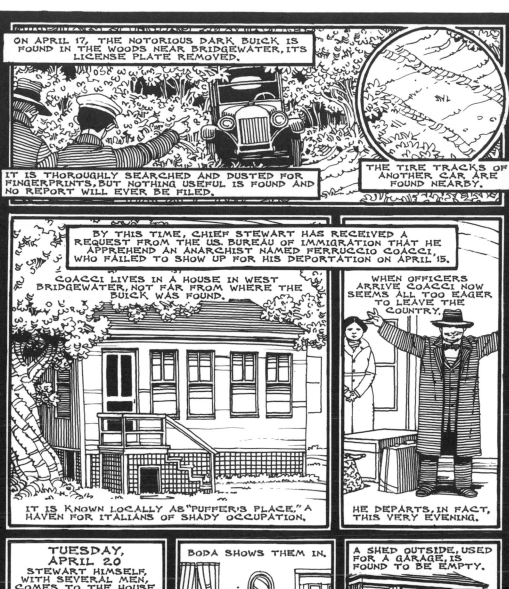

ON APRIL 17, THE NOTORIOUS DARK BUICK IS FOUND IN THE WOODS NEAR BRIDGEWATER, ITS LICENSE PLATE REMOVED.

IT IS THOROUGHLY SEARCHED AND DUSTED FOR FINGERPRINTS, BUT NOTHING USEFUL IS FOUND AND NO REPORT WILL EVER BE FILED.

THE TIRE TRACKS OF ANOTHER CAR ARE FOUND NEARBY.

BY THIS TIME, CHIEF STEWART HAS RECEIVED A REQUEST FROM THE US. BUREAU OF IMMIGRATION THAT HE APPREHEND AN ANARCHIST NAMED FERRUCCIO COACCI WHO FAILED TO SHOW UP FOR HIS DEPORTATION ON APRIL '15.

COACCI LIVES IN A HOUSE IN WEST BRIDGEWATER, NOT FAR FROM WHERE THE BUICK WAS FOUND.

WHEN OFFICERS ARRIVE COACCI NOW SEEMS ALL TOO EAGER TO LEAVE THE COUNTRY.

IT IS KNOWN LOCALLY AS "PUFFER'S PLACE," A HAVEN FOR ITALIANS OF SHADY OCCUPATION.

HE DEPARTS, IN FACT, THIS VERY EVENING.

TUESDAY, APRIL 20
STEWART HIMSELF, WITH SEVERAL MEN, COMES TO THE HOUSE.

THEY ARE GREETED BY A MAN CALLING HIMSELF MIKE BODA.

BODA SHOWS THEM IN.

A SEARCH FINDS NOTHING IN THE HOUSE CONNECTED TO THE CRIMES.

A SHED OUTSIDE, USED FOR A GARAGE, IS FOUND TO BE EMPTY.

BODA SAYS THAT HIS CAR, A 1914 OVERLAND, IS IN THE SHOP FOR REPAIRS.

AFTER HIS VISIT, STEWART LEARNS THAT MIKE BODA IS ACTUALLY THE ANARCHIST MARIO BUDA, WELL-KNOWN TO THE FEDERAL AUTHORITIES AS A SKILLED BOMB-MAKER.

THE CHIEF IS NOW CERTAIN THAT THE GANG HE IS AFTER OPERATES OUT OF THIS HOUSE.

BUT WHEN HE RETURNS TWO DAYS LATER, HE FINDS IT COMPLETELY CLEARED OUT, ITS RESIDENTS VANISHED.

STEWART LOCATES THE GARAGE, AT ELM SQUARE IN WEST BRIDGEWATER, WHERE BUDA'S CAR REMAINS UNDER REPAIR.

JOHNSON AUTO REPA

HERE HE INSTRUCTS THE OWNER, SIMON JOHNSON, TO CALL HIM WHEN BUDA COMES FOR THE CAR.

BROCKTON

BUICK FOUND

WEST BRIDGEWATER

"PUFFER'S PLACE"

ELM SQ.

BRI

WEDNESDAY, MAY 5 AT 9:30PM THE CALL COMES.

FOUR MEN HAVE ARRIVED AT THE JOHNSON HOME TO CLAIM THE OVERLAND.

BUT STEWART ARRIVES TOO LATE: THE MEN ARE GONE.

ACCORDING TO JOHNSON, THEY DECIDED NOT TO TAKE THE CAR, SINCE ITS LICENSE PLATE HAD EXPIRED.

BUDA AND ANOTHER MAN DEPARTED ON A MOTORCYCLE.

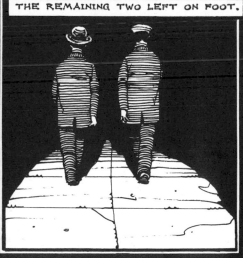

THE REMAINING TWO LEFT ON FOOT.

THESE TWO UNKNOWN MEN WALK NORTHWARD FOR ABOUT ONE MILE.

AND THEN BOARD A STREETCAR.

AT ABOUT 10:00PM, IN THE TOWN OF BROCKTON, OFFICER MICHAEL CONNOLLY BOARDS THE CAR.

HE APPROACHES THE TWO MEN AND PLACES THEM UNDER ARREST AS "SUSPICIOUS CHARACTERS."

PART II

THE ACCUSED

THE PRISONERS IDENTIFY THEMSELVES AS:
BARTOLOMEO VANZETTI, AGE 31, AND
NICOLA SACCO, AGE 29. BOTH ARE GAINFULLY
EMPLOYED AND HAVE NO CRIMINAL RECORDS.

WHO ARE THESE MEN? WHAT BROUGHT THEM TO THIS
PIVOTAL MOMENT? A REVIEW OF THEIR LIVES THUS FAR:

BARTOLOMEO VANZETTI WAS BORN JUNE 11, 1888, IN THE VILLAGE OF VILLAFALLETTO IN NORTHERN ITALY.

FROM AN EARLY AGE, HE WORKED AS AN APPRENTICE BAKER AND CANDY-MAKER IN THE TOWNS OF CAVOUR AND TURIN.

AFTER THE DEATH OF HIS MOTHER, HE EMIGRATED TO AMERICA, ARRIVING AT ELLIS ISLAND IN 1908.

HE RENOUNCED THE CATHOLIC FAITH AND COMMITTED HIMSELF TO SOCIALISM.

VANZETTI EMBARKED UPON A LIFE OF MANUAL LABOR ON THE FARMS, STONE QUARRIES, BRICK YARDS, HIGHWAYS AND RAILROADS OF NEW ENGLAND.

IN MASSACHUSETTS, HE WORKED AT THE PLYMOUTH CORDAGE CO. WHERE HIS INVOLVEMENT IN A 1916 STRIKE MARKED HIM AS A LABOR AGITATOR.

AT PRESENT HE SELLS FISH FROM HIS PUSH-CART ON THE STREETS OF PLYMOUTH.

KNOWN AS A GENTLE AND POETIC SOUL, HE IS A FAMILIAR AND BELOVED PRESENCE IN THE ITALIAN COMMUNITY.

WITHOUT A WIFE OR ANY CLOSE ATTACHMENTS, HE LIVES ALONE IN A SMALL RENTED ROOM.

NICOLA SACCO WAS BORN APRIL 22, 1891 IN THE SOUTHERN ITALIAN VILLAGE OF TORREMAGGIORE.

HE HAD LITTLE FORMAL SCHOOLING BUT GREW UP WITH A LOVE OF NATURE AND THE OUTDOORS.

HIS OLDER BROTHER SABINO WAS A CONSTANT COMPANION. TOGETHER THEY EMIGRATED TO AMERICA, LANDING IN BOSTON IN APRIL OF 1908.

AS HE WORKED AT A SERIES OF LABORING JOBS, SACCO TURNED HIS SYMPATHIES TO THE SOCIALIST MOVEMENT.

HE AND HIS WIFE ROSINA (WHOM HE WED IN 1912.) PRESENTED PROGRAMS TO RAISE FUNDS FOR STRIKERS.

THEIR SON DANTE WAS BORN IN 1914.

AT PRESENT HE WORKS AT THE 3K SHOE FACTORY IN STOUGHTON IN THE SKILLED POSITION OF EDGE-TRIMMER.

HE AND HIS FAMILY OCCUPY A SMALL HOUSE ON THE PROPERTY OF THE FACTORY'S OWNER MICHAEL KELLEY.

HERE, IN HIS SPARE HOURS, HE TENDS A LARGE FLOWER AND VEGETABLE GARDEN.

SACCO AND VANZETTI ARE KNOWN TO HAVE MET AT A BOSTON ANARCHIST CONCLAVE IN MAY OF 1917...

HE WORLD ONITE!
CIALISM O WAR!

SHORTLY AFTER THE UNITED STATES ENTERED THE WORLD WAR.

THEIR LEADER, LUIGI GALLEANI, IS A PROPONENT OF DIRECT ACTION.

HIS SECT ADVOCATES BOMBING AND ASSASSINATION AS TOOLS ON THE PEOPLES' STRUGGLE.

DESPITE SUCH VIOLENT ELEMENTS, THE ANARCHIST PHILOSOPHY HOLDS THAT HUMANITY CAN LIVE IN FREEDOM AND HARMONY ONCE IT IS DIVESTED OF ITS OPPRESSIVE INSTITUTIONS.

IN JUNE SEVERAL OF THE GALLEANISTI EMIGRATE TO MEXICO. SACCO AND VANZETTI AND ABOUT 60 OF THEIR COMRADES SETTLE IN THE CITY OF MONTERREY IN PREPARATION FOR A RETURN TO ITALY.

TEXAS

MONTERREY

EXICO

GULF
ME

THE GROUP ALSO INCLUDES THE BOMB-BUILDERS MARIO BUDA AND CARLO VALDINOCCI AND THE WRITER AND EDITOR ANDREA SALSEDO.

THEIR PLAN IS TO FOMENT AN UPRISING IN THEIR NATIVE LAND ALONG THE LINES OF THE RECENT SOCIALIST REVOLUTION IN RUSSIA.

THEIR RESIDENCE IN MEXICO ALLOWS THEM THE FURTHER ADVANTAGE OF AVOIDING CONSCRIPTION IN THE "RICH MAN'S WAR."

IN SEPTEMBER, AFTER A SWELTERING SUMMER IN THEIR ADOBE HUTS, THE DISPIRITED REVOLUTIONARIES RETURN TO THE UNITED STATES.

BOTH SACCO AND VANZETTI DONATE TO AND DISTRIBUTE THE NEW YORK-BASED ANARCHIST NEWSPAPER, CRONACA SOVVERSIVA, EDITED BY ANDREA SALSEDO.

VANZETTI ALSO CONTRIBUTES THE OCCASIONAL ARTICLE.

DURING THIS TIME, BOTH MEN APPEAR IN THE GOVERNMENT'S SIGHTS AS DANGEROUS RADICALS.

BY THE EARLY DAYS OF 1919, WITH THE END OF THE WAR, THE BOLSHEVIKS ENTRENCHED IN RUSSIA, AND UNREST GROWING IN MANY COUNTRIES...

FEAR OF WORLDWIDE REVOLUTION IS RAMPANT.

IN AMERICA A FULL-BLOWN RED SCARE ERUPTS.

THE GOVERNMENT INITIATES A CAMPAIGN OF HARASSMENT AND REPRESSION.

WEDNESDAY, APRIL 30, 1919
THE U.S. POST OFFICE FOILS A PLOT THAT WOULD HAVE SENT BOMBS TO MORE THAN 30 PEOPLE ON AN ANARCHIST ENEMIES LIST.

THEY INCLUDE: J. P. MORGAN, JR., JOHN D. ROCKEFELLER, AND THE U.S. ATTORNEY GENERAL A. MITCHELL PALMER.

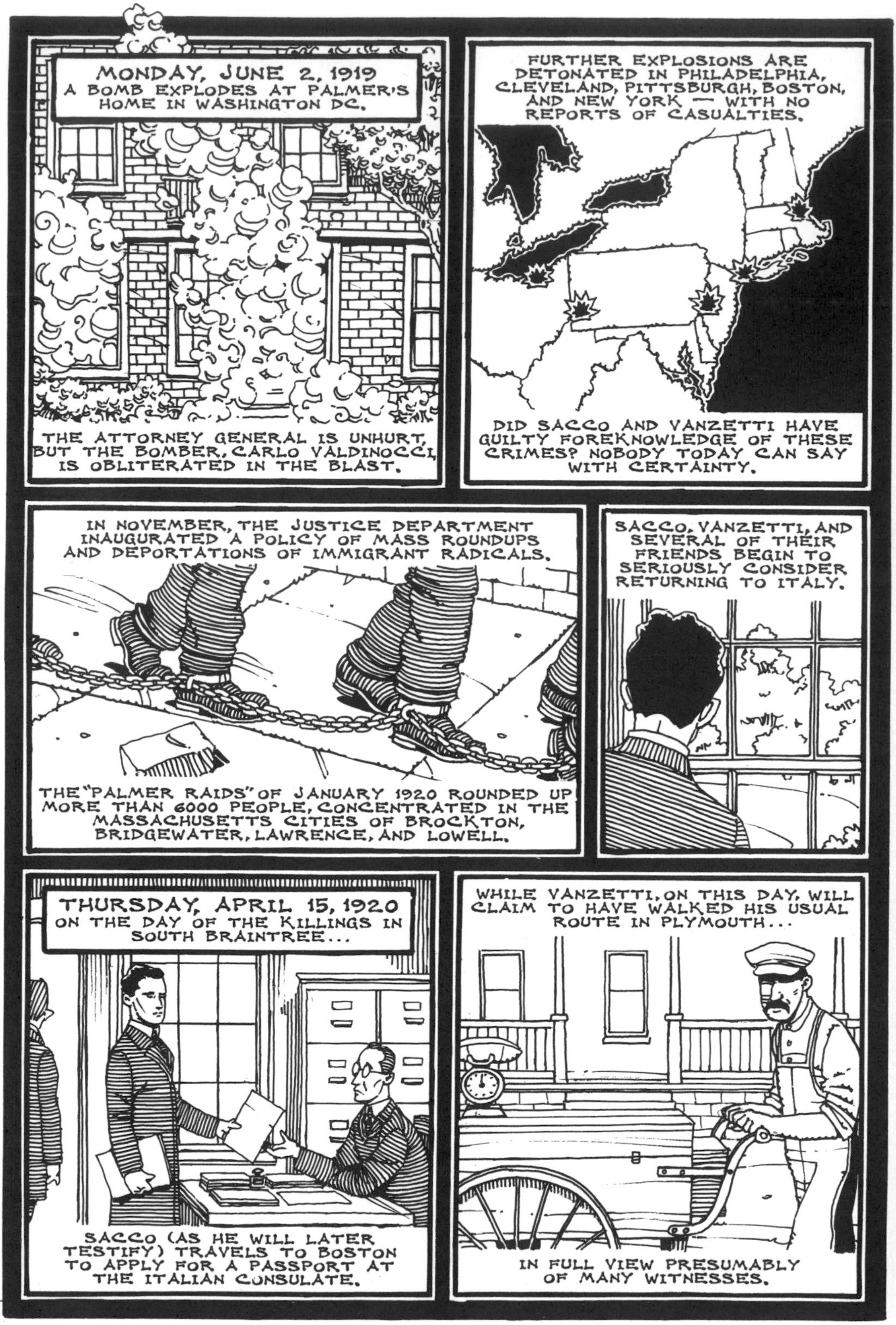
MONDAY, JUNE 2, 1919
A BOMB EXPLODES AT PALMER'S HOME IN WASHINGTON DC.
THE ATTORNEY GENERAL IS UNHURT, BUT THE BOMBER, CARLO VALDINOCCI, IS OBLITERATED IN THE BLAST.
FURTHER EXPLOSIONS ARE DETONATED IN PHILADELPHIA, CLEVELAND, PITTSBURGH, BOSTON, AND NEW YORK — WITH NO REPORTS OF CASUALTIES.
DID SACCO AND VANZETTI HAVE GUILTY FOREKNOWLEDGE OF THESE CRIMES? NOBODY TODAY CAN SAY WITH CERTAINTY.
IN NOVEMBER, THE JUSTICE DEPARTMENT INAUGURATED A POLICY OF MASS ROUNDUPS AND DEPORTATIONS OF IMMIGRANT RADICALS.
THE "PALMER RAIDS" OF JANUARY 1920 ROUNDED UP MORE THAN 6000 PEOPLE, CONCENTRATED IN THE MASSACHUSETTS CITIES OF BROCKTON, BRIDGEWATER, LAWRENCE, AND LOWELL.
SACCO, VANZETTI, AND SEVERAL OF THEIR FRIENDS BEGIN TO SERIOUSLY CONSIDER RETURNING TO ITALY.
THURSDAY, APRIL 15, 1920
ON THE DAY OF THE KILLINGS IN SOUTH BRAINTREE...
SACCO (AS HE WILL LATER TESTIFY) TRAVELS TO BOSTON TO APPLY FOR A PASSPORT AT THE ITALIAN CONSULATE.
WHILE VANZETTI, ON THIS DAY, WILL CLAIM TO HAVE WALKED HIS USUAL ROUTE IN PLYMOUTH...
IN FULL VIEW PRESUMABLY OF MANY WITNESSES.

MONDAY, MARCH 8, 1920
THE BROOKLYN PRINT SHOP OF CRONACA SOVVERSIVA IS RAIDED BY AGENTS OF THE JUSTICE DEPARTMENT.

ANDREA SALSEDO AND ROBERTO ELIA ARE PLACED UNDER ARREST AND INTERROGATED AT THE DEPARTMENT'S NEW YORK OFFICE ON PARK ROW.

SUNDAY, MAY 2
SALSEDO DIES IN A MYSTERIOUS FALL FROM THE 14TH FLOOR OF THE PARK ROW BUILDING.

ON A VISIT TO NEW YORK THE NEXT DAY, VANZETTI LEARNS OF HIS FRIEND'S DEATH. WAS IT AN ACCIDENT? SUICIDE? MURDER?

FEARING A NEW ROUND OF ARRESTS AND DEPORTATIONS, HE TAKES THE TRAIN TO SACCO'S HOME IN STOUGHTON.

THE MEN PLAN A COURSE OF ACTION: THEY MUST WARN THEIR ASSOCIATES TO GO UNDERGROUND AND DESTROY ALL INCRIMINATING LITERATURE.

TO REACH THEIR FAR-FLUNG COMRADES THEY WILL NEED AN AUTOMOBILE.

WEDNESDAY, MAY 5
AS IT HAPPENS, MARIO BUDA'S CAR IS READY TO BE PICKED UP IN BRIDGEWATER.

AT 9:00, SACCO AND VANZETTI ARRIVE BY STREETCAR.

AT THE GARAGE, THEY MEET BUDA, WHO HAS COME BY MOTORCYCLE, ACCOMPANIED BY A FOURTH ANARCHIST RICCARDO ORCIANI.

FINDING THE REPAIR SHOP CLOSED, THEY GO TO THE NEARBY HOME OF SIMON JOHNSON.

THE MECHANIC SUGGESTS THAT THEY MIGHT NOT WANT THE CAR SINCE ITS LICENSE PLATE, HAVING EXPIRED, HAS BEEN REMOVED.

JOHNSON'S WIFE RUTH WALKS TO THE HOUSE NEXT DOOR, ON THE PRETEXT OF BORROWING A CAN OF MILK.

WHILE THERE, SHE TELEPHONES THE POLICE.

UPON HER RETURN, THE FOUR VISITORS SEEM SUSPICIOUS, AGITATED.

DECIDING NOT TO TAKE THE CAR, THEY DEPART

SACCO AND VANZETTI, AFTER WALKING FOR ABOUT A MILE, BOARD A NORTHBOUND STREETCAR

WHERE, AT A STOP IN BROCKTON, AT 10:00PM, THEY ARE PLACED UNDER ARREST.

THE PRISONERS ARE BROUGHT TO THE BRIDGEWATER POLICE STATION.

THEY ARE NOT TOLD WHY THEY ARE IN CUSTODY.

BOTH ARE FOUND TO BE WELL ARMED.

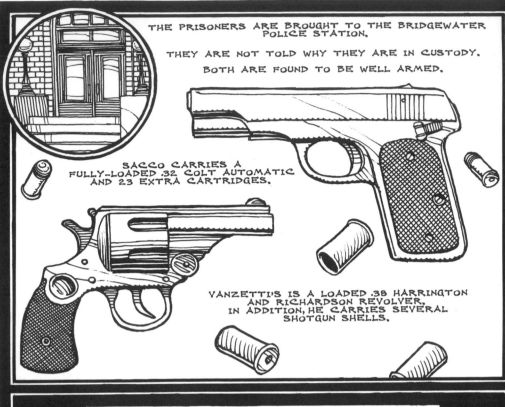

SACCO CARRIES A FULLY-LOADED .32 COLT AUTOMATIC AND 23 EXTRA CARTRIDGES.

VANZETTI'S IS A LOADED .38 HARRINGTON AND RICHARDSON REVOLVER. IN ADDITION, HE CARRIES SEVERAL SHOTGUN SHELLS.

THE TWO ARE SEPARATED AND UNDERGO INTENSE QUESTIONING BY CHIEF STEWART. IN THEIR FEAR AND NERVOUSNESS THEY TELL ONE LIE AFTER ANOTHER.

NO THEY WERE NEVER AT SIMON JOHNSON'S HOUSE IN BRIDGEWATER.

THEY DO NOT KNOW MARIO BUDA.

THEY SAW NO ONE ON A MOTORCYCLE.

THEY ARE NOT ANARCHISTS.

SACCO, PERHAPS OUT OF CONFUSION, CLAIMS TO HAVE BEEN AT WORK ALL DAY ON APRIL 15.

STEWART NOW BELIEVES THAT HE HAS FOUND THE FIVE MEN RESPONSIBLE FOR BOTH THE BRIDGEWATER ATTEMPTED ROBBERY AND THE KILLINGS IN SOUTH BRAINTREE: TWO ARE IN CUSTODY; ANOTHER, COACCI, IS IN ITALY; BUDA AND ORCIANI REMAIN AT LARGE.

ON HIS FIRST NIGHT IN JAIL, AS HE WILL LATER TESTIFY, VANZETTI IS VISITED OUTSIDE HIS CELL BY A POLICEMAN, WHO SLOWLY LOADS HIS PISTOL, AIMS AT HIM, AND PRETENDS TO FIRE.

THURSDAY, MAY 6
SACCO AND VANZETTI ARE BOOKED FOR CARRYING CONCEALED WEAPONS AND HELD WITHOUT BAIL.

SOME 24 EYEWITNESSES FROM BOTH CRIME SCENES ARE BROUGHT IN TO VIEW THEM IN THEIR SEPARATE CELLS.

CONTRARY TO ACCEPTED PROCEDURE, THE PRISONERS ARE NOT PLACED IN A LINE-UP.

SACCO, IN FACT, IS ORDERED TO CROUCH INTO A SHOOTING POSTURE.

SEVERAL WITNESSES IDENTIFY BOTH MEN AS THE BANDITS, BUT MOST OF THEM CANNOT MAKE A POSITIVE IDENTIFICATION.

SEARCHES OF BOTH MEN'S HOMES FIND STACKS OF ANTI-AMERICAN LITERATURE.

IRONICALLY THEY FAILED TO HIDE THE VERY MATERIAL THAT THEY WERE SET ON WARNING OTHERS ABOUT.

FRIDAY, JUNE 11
ON THE STRENGTH OF THE EYEWITNESSES, AND THE FACT THAT HE CARRIED SHOTGUN SHELLS, VANZETTI IS INDICTED FOR THE ATTEMPTED ROBBERY IN BRIDGEWATER.

HE IS KEPT IN JAIL IN PLYMOUTH, WHILE SACCO IS TRANSPORTED TO THE NORFOLK COUNTY JAIL IN DEDHAM.

TUESDAY, JUNE 22, VANZETTI'S TRIAL OPENS AT THE PLYMOUTH COUNTY COURTHOUSE.

THE JUDGE, WEBSTER THAYER, IS WELL-KNOWN FOR HIS ANTIPATHY TOWARD IMMIGRANTS AND RADICALS.

FOR THE COMMONWEALTH: THE DISTRICT ATTORNEY FOR PLYMOUTH AND NORFOLK COUNTIES, FREDERICK G. KATZMANN.

FOR THE DEFENSE: JOHN P. VAHEY.

A HANDFUL OF WITNESSES POSITIVELY IDENTIFY VANZETTI AS THE "SHOTGUN BANDIT."

THE DEFENSE OFFERS 21 CITIZENS WHO RECALL BUYING EELS FROM HIM ON CHRISTMAS EVE.

BUT ALL OF THEM ARE ITALIAN, WITH LITTLE COMMAND OF ENGLISH, AND END UP BEING DISCOUNTED BY THE JURY.

THURSDAY, JULY 1 VANZETTI IS FOUND GUILTY OF ASSAULT WITH INTENT TO ROB AND ASSAULT WITH INTENT TO MURDER.

HIS SENTENCE IS 15-20 YEARS IN PRISON A STEEP PENALTY FOR A FIRST OFFENSE.

AS A CONVICTED FELON HE IS TAKEN TO THE STATE PRISON IN CHARLESTOWN.

SATURDAY, SEPTEMBER 11 SACCO AND VANZETTI ARE INDICTED FOR MURDER IN THE SOUTH BRAINTREE ROBBERY.

AS FOR THE OTHER SUSPECTS: COACCI AND ORCIANI ARE CLEARED OF INVOLVEMENT. ONLY MARIO BUDA REMAINS AT LARGE.

THURSDAY, SEPTEMBER 16 AT 12 NOON A LARGE BOMB EXPLODES ON WALL STREET IN NEW YORK CITY.

38 CITIZENS ARE KILLED AND ABOUT 200 WOUNDED.

THE PERPETRATOR IS MOST LIKELY...MARIO BUDA, IN REVENGE FOR THE INDICTMENTS.

...CRET SERVICE - LUI... ...VIOLENT GROUP IN AMERIC... ...ND DIRECT PROOF OF LEA...

THE BOSTON HERALD PUBLISHES PHOTOS OF THE DESTRUCTION ALONGSIDE MUG SHOTS OF THE PRISONERS.

PART III

THE CASE FOR THE COMMONWEALTH

TUESDAY, MAY 31, 1921
THE TRIAL OF SACCO AND VANZETTI OPENS AT
THE NORFOLK COUNTY COURTHOUSE IN DEDHAM.

IN KEEPING WITH THE CURRENT STATE OF PUBLIC
HYSTERIA, THE BUILDING IS PATROLLED BY 22 ARMED
GUARDS AS WELL AS FEDERAL AGENTS AND THE STATE
BOMB SQUAD.

THE PACKED COURTROOM IS CALLED TO ORDER BY JUDGE WEBSTER THAYER.

(AFTER PRESIDING AT VANZETTI'S TRIAL IN PLYMOUTH THE JURIST SPECIFICALLY REQUESTED TO BE ASSIGNED THIS ONE.)

THE DEFENDANTS ARE PLACED IN WHAT AMOUNTS TO A CAGE IN THE CENTER OF THE ROOM.

THE PROSECUTOR IS ONCE AGAIN THE DISTRICT ATTORNEY FREDERICK KATZMANN.

HE IS ASSISTED BY HAROLD P. WILLIAMS.

THE DEFENSE IS LED BY THE FLAMBOYANT FRED H. MOORE OF LOS ANGELES...

A DEDICATED LEFTIST, KNOWN FOR HIS DEFENSE OF LABOR UNIONS AGAINST CHARGES OF SEDITION AND DRAFT-DODGING.

HE HAS BEEN RECRUITED BY THE ANARCHIST LEADER CARLO TRESCA AND THE ACTIVISTS ELIZABETH GURLEY FLYNN AND MARY HEATON VORSE.

TRESCA

FLYNN

VORSE

A DEFENSE COMMITTEE FOR THE ACCUSED HAS BEEN ESTABLISHED...

ORGANIZED BY VANZETTI'S FRIEND ALDO FELICANI.

IT OPERATES OUT OF A CRAMPED OFFICE ON BATTERY STREET IN NORTH BOSTON.

MOORE IS ASSISTED BY WILLIAM CALLAHAN (FOR SACCO)

AND THE BROTHERS JEREMIAH AND THOMAS McANARNY (FOR VANZETTI).

THE FIRST ORDER OF BUSINESS IS THE SELECTION OF A JURY.

OF THE 500 MEN IN THE INITIAL JURY POOL, ONLY SEVEN ARE DEEMED ACCEPTABLE TO BOTH SIDES.

TO SECURE THE REMAINING JURORS JUDGE THAYER DIRECTS THE SHERIFF TO SUMMON "ADDITIONAL CITIZENS FROM THE BYSTANDERS OR FROM THE COUNTY AT LARGE."

WHEN COURT ADJOURNS, DEPUTIES SCOUR THE COUNTY AND ROUND UP 175 MORE MEN.

THE NEXT MORNING THE JURY PANEL IS COMPLETE.

A GROCER, A MASON, TWO MACHINISTS, A FARMER, A RETIRED POLICE CHIEF, TWO FACTORY WORKERS, A PHOTOGRAPHER, A STORE CLERK, AND TWO REAL ESTATE AGENTS.

THEY ARE TAKEN, FIRST OF ALL, ON A TOUR OF THE LOCATIONS RELEVANT TO THE CASE:

THE CRIME SCENE IN SOUTH BRAINTREE, "PUFFER'S PLACE" IN WEST BRIDGEWATER, THE WOODS WHERE THE BUICK WAS FOUND, THE GARAGE OF SIMON JOHNSON.

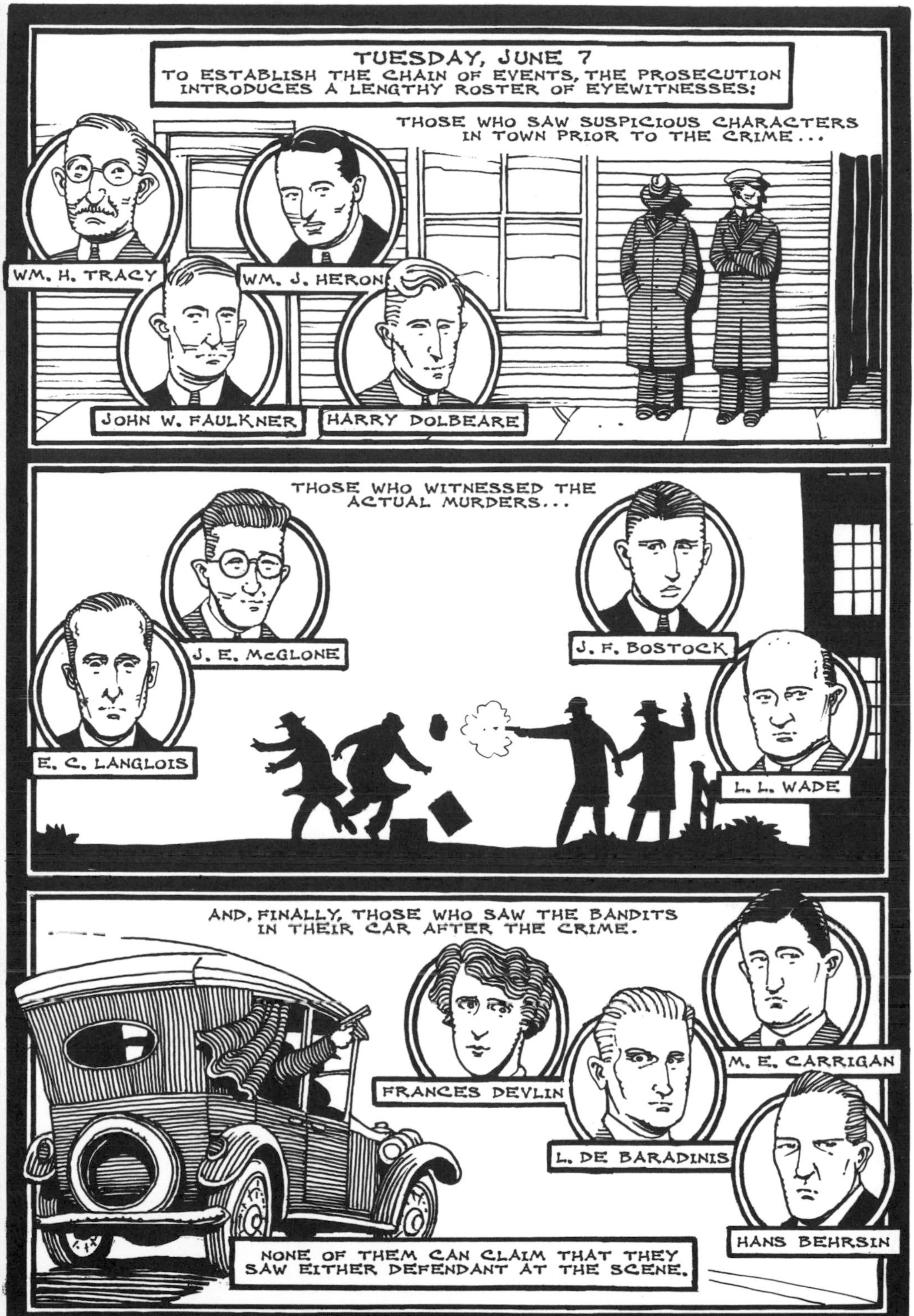
TUESDAY, JUNE 7
TO ESTABLISH THE CHAIN OF EVENTS, THE PROSECUTION INTRODUCES A LENGTHY ROSTER OF EYEWITNESSES:
THOSE WHO SAW SUSPICIOUS CHARACTERS IN TOWN PRIOR TO THE CRIME...
WM. H. TRACY
WM. J. HERON
JOHN W. FAULKNER
HARRY DOLBEARE
THOSE WHO WITNESSED THE ACTUAL MURDERS...
J. E. McGLONE
E. C. LANGLOIS
J. F. BOSTOCK
L. L. WADE
AND, FINALLY, THOSE WHO SAW THE BANDITS IN THEIR CAR AFTER THE CRIME.
FRANCES DEVLIN
M. E. CARRIGAN
L. DE BARADINIS
HANS BEHRSIN
NONE OF THEM CAN CLAIM THAT THEY SAW EITHER DEFENDANT AT THE SCENE.

SIX KEY WITNESSES, HOWEVER, OFFER POSITIVE AND UNSHAKABLE IDENTIFICATIONS. STILL, THEY ARE NOT WITHOUT THEIR PROBLEMS.

MICHAEL LEVANGIE: THE RAIL CROSSING ATTENDANT ON PEARL STREET IDENTIFIES VANZETTI AS THE DRIVER WHO POINTED A GUN AT HIM.

VANZETTI, HOWEVER, CANNOT DRIVE A CAR.

AUSTIN REED: THE CROSSING ATTENDANT AT MATFIELD CLAIMS THAT THE MAN WHO SHOUTED AT HIM IN UNACCENTED ENGLISH WAS VANZETTI.

WHAT ARE YOU HOLDING US UP FOR?

BUT VANZETTI, AS EVERYONE KNOWS, CANNOT SPEAK CLEAR ENGLISH.

MRS. LOLA ANDREWS: WALKING ALONG PEARL ST. ON THE MORNING OF THE CRIME, TALKED WITH TWO MEN AT WORK ON A CAR. ONE OF THEM WAS SACCO.

BUT SHE HAS TOLD OTHERS THAT SHE COULD NOT IDENTIFY THE MEN AND FAILED TO RECOGNIZE A PHOTOGRAPH OF SACCO.

LOUIS PELSER: SAW THE MURDERS FROM A WINDOW IN THE RICE & HUTCHINS FACTORY AND SAYS THAT SACCO IS THE "DEAD IMAGE" OF THE SHOOTER.

BUT HIS CO-WORKERS RECALL THAT HE DUCKED BELOW THE WINDOW WHEN THE SHOOTING STARTED.

MARY E. SPLAINE: FROM HER WINDOW IN SLATER & MORRILL'S BUILDING #1, SAW THE MAN IN THE BACK SEAT OF THE GETAWAY CAR AND SWEARS IT WAS SACCO.

BUT SHE SAW THE CAR FOR NO LONGER THAN A FEW SECONDS FROM 80 FEET AWAY.

CARLOS GOODRICH: IN A POOLROOM ON PEARL ST. HEARD THE SHOTS AND SAW THE CAR SPEED BY. THE MAN FIRING FROM THE BACK SEAT WAS SACCO.

BUT GOODRICH HAS A POOR REPUTATION FOR TRUTHFULNESS AND MADE EARLIER CONTRADICTORY STATEMENTS.

THE NEXT PHASE OF THE COMMONWEALTH CASE INVOLVES THE DEFENDANTS' CONSCIOUSNESS OF GUILT. ON THE NIGHT OF THEIR ARREST THEY:

CARRIED LOADED PISTOLS AND EXTRA AMMUNITION ON THEIR PERSONS...

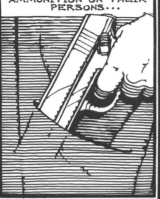

TOOK FLIGHT WHEN MRS. JOHNSON CALLED THE POLICE...

LIED TO AUTHORITIES ABOUT THEIR ACTIVITIES AND ASSOCIATIONS.

OFFICER CONOLLY, WHO RODE WITH THE PAIR TO THE BROCKTON POLICE STATION, TESTIFIES THAT BOTH MEN MOTIONED FOR THEIR GUNS...

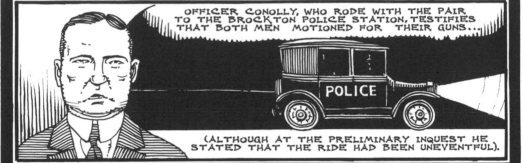

POLICE

(ALTHOUGH AT THE PRELIMINARY INQUEST HE STATED THAT THE RIDE HAD BEEN UNEVENTFUL).

VANZETTI JUMPS UP WITH UNEXPECTED FURY.

YOU ARE A LIAR!

FRED MOORE IS LIKEWISE ON HIS FEET OFTEN, MAKING OBJECTION AFTER OBJECTION...

IRRITATING THE JUDGE WHO CONTEMPTUOUSLY OVERRULES HIM IN EVERY INSTANCE

THE DEFENSE IS CAUGHT BY SURPRISE WHEN KATZMANN INTRODUCES INTO EVIDENCE A CAP FOUND AT THE CRIME SCENE...

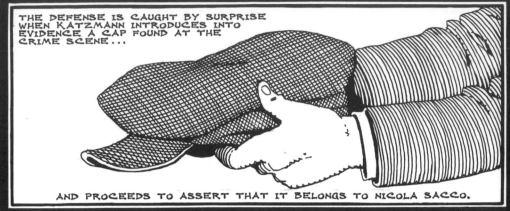

AND PROCEEDS TO ASSERT THAT IT BELONGS TO NICOLA SACCO.

WITNESSES DESCRIBED THE SHOOTER AS WEARING A CAP...

YET THE MAN FIRING FROM THE GETAWAY CAR WAS WITHOUT ONE.

SACCO'S EMPLOYER, G. T. KELLEY, TESTIFIES THAT THE CAP SOMEWHAT RESEMBLES THE ONE WORN TO WORK BY THE ITALIAN.

IN FACT THE CAP IN EVIDENCE HAS A TEAR IN THE BACK OF THE LINING...

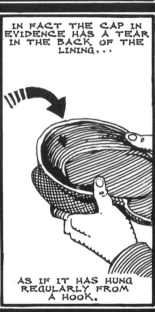

AS IF IT HAS HUNG REGULARLY FROM A HOOK.

THE DEFENSE CALLS INTO QUESTION THE WORTH OF AN EXHIBIT THAT COULD HAVE BEEN LOST BY ANYBODY IN THE CROWD THAT JAMMED PEARL STREET.

AS A RESULT THIS POINT REMAINS A MINOR ONE FOR THE COMMONWEALTH CASE.

THEIR NEXT POINT INVOLVES THE HARRINGTON & RICHARDSON REVOLVER RECOVERED FROM VANZETTI.

IS IT THE GUN OF THE FALLEN GUARD BERARDELLI?

THIS IS CONSIDERED THE STRONGEST EVIDENCE AGAINST VANZETTI SINCE THERE IS LITTLE ELSE TO PLACE HIM AT THE SCENE.

BERARDELLI WAS KNOWN TO CARRY A SNUB-NOSED .38 REVOLVER BUT IT WAS NOT FOUND ON HIS BODY.

NO WITNESS HOWEVER SAW THE BANDITS TAKE A PISTOL FROM THE GUARD.

IN MARCH OF 1920 BERARDELLI TOOK HIS REVOLVER TO IVER & JOHNSON SPORTING GOODS IN BOSTON FOR REPAIR WORK.

BUT WAS IT EVER RETURNED TO HIM?

A CLERK FROM THE STORE PRODUCES PAPERWORK SHOWING THAT THE GUARD TURNED IN A .38 H&R REVOLVER FOR REPAIR OF THE HAMMER.

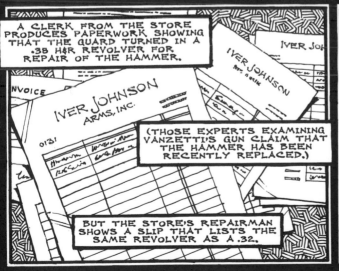

IVER JOHNSON
ARMS, INC.

(THOSE EXPERTS EXAMINING VANZETTI'S GUN CLAIM THAT THE HAMMER HAS BEEN RECENTLY REPLACED.)

BUT THE STORE'S REPAIRMAN SHOWS A SLIP THAT LISTS THE SAME REVOLVER AS A .32.

IN ANY CASE THE GUN IS NO LONGER IN THE STORE AND THERE IS NO RECORD OF IT HAVING BEEN RETRIEVED.

THE QUESTION OF THIS REVOLVER REMAINS FRUSTRATINGLY UNRESOLVED.

KATZMANN RESERVES HIS MOST COMPELLING EVIDENCE FOR LAST, AS HE INTRODUCES HIS FIREARMS EXPERTS:

STATE POLICE CAPTAIN WILLIAM PROCTOR...

AND U.S. ARMY CAPTAIN CHARLES VAN AMBURGH, TECHNICAL ADVISOR TO SEVERAL FIREARMS MANUFACTURERS.

THE FOUR BULLETS REMOVED FROM THE VICTIM BERARDELLI HAVE BEEN NUMBERED I THROUGH IV BY THE CORONER DR. McGRATH.

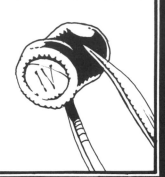

IN ADDITION, FOUR EJECTED SHELLS WERE PICKED UP FROM THE STREET BY A WITNESS AND KEPT IN A DESK AT THE SHOE FACTORY, BEFORE BEING TURNED OVER TO POLICE.

OF THESE FOUR, TWO ARE PETERS SHELLS, ONE IS A REMINGTON, AND ONE IS A WINCHESTER OF AN OBSOLETE TYPE.

OF THE 23 BULLETS FOUND IN SACCO'S POCKET UPON HIS ARREST...

16 ARE PETERS, 3 ARE REMINGTON, AND 4 ARE WINCHESTER OF THE SAME OBSOLETE TYPE

BULLETS I II & IV, AS WELL AS THE TWO REMOVED FROM PARMENTER, ARE SHOWN TO HAVE A CLOCKWISE, OR RIGHT TWIST, TO THEIR RIFLING.

CAPT. PROCTOR TESTIFIES THAT THESE FIVE WERE FIRED FROM A SAVAGE AUTOMATIC...

A GUN THAT HAS NOT BEEN (NOR EVER WILL BE) RECOVERED.

BULLET III, HOWEVER, HAS A COUNTER-CLOCKWISE OR LEFT TWIST...

AND SO WAS OBVIOUSLY FIRED FROM A DIFFERENT WEAPON.

IN EARLY JUNE, IN THE TOWN OF LOWELL, SACCO'S COLT AUTOMATIC WAS FIRED 14 TIMES INTO A BOX OF SAWDUST...

AND THE BULLETS EXAMINED MICROSCOPICALLY BY EXPERTS FROM BOTH SIDES.

HAVE THE PROSECUTION EXPERTS CONCLUDED THAT BULLET III WAS FIRED FROM SACCO'S PISTOL?

PROCTOR:

MY OPINION IS THAT IT IS CONSISTENT WITH BEING FIRED FROM THAT PISTOL.

VAN AMBURGH:

I AM INCLINED TO BELIEVE THAT NUMBER III BULLET WAS FIRED FROM THIS COLT AUTOMATIC.

BOTH MEN ALSO ASSERT THAT THE SINGLE WINCHESTER SHELL FOUND AT THE SCENE (SHELL W), MARKED BY THE INDENTATION OF THE FIRING PIN, IS "CONSISTENT WITH" A COLT AUTOMATIC.

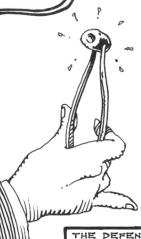

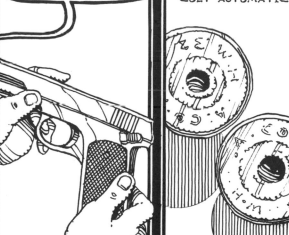

THE DEFENSE, ON CROSS-EXAMINATION, FAILS TO CALL ATTENTION TO THESE EQUIVOCAL RESPONSES.

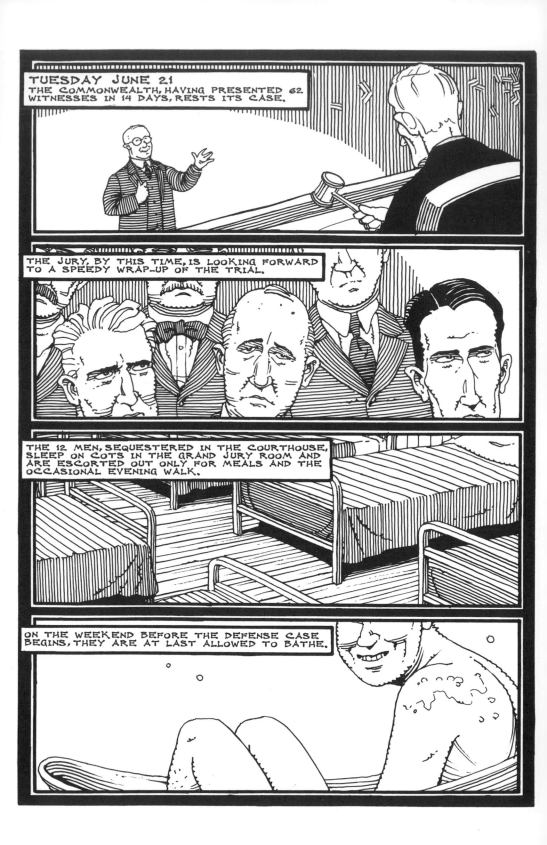

TUESDAY JUNE 21
THE COMMONWEALTH, HAVING PRESENTED 62 WITNESSES IN 14 DAYS, RESTS ITS CASE.

THE JURY, BY THIS TIME, IS LOOKING FORWARD TO A SPEEDY WRAP-UP OF THE TRIAL.

THE 12 MEN, SEQUESTERED IN THE COURTHOUSE, SLEEP ON COTS IN THE GRAND JURY ROOM AND ARE ESCORTED OUT ONLY FOR MEALS AND THE OCCASIONAL EVENING WALK.

ON THE WEEKEND BEFORE THE DEFENSE CASE BEGINS, THEY ARE AT LAST ALLOWED TO BATHE.

PART IV

THE CASE FOR
THE DEFENSE

WEDNESDAY, JUNE 22, 1921
FRED MOORE OPENS THE CASE FOR THE DEFENSE.

THE ERRATIC ATTORNEY WILL NOW, UNFORTUNATELY, ONLY
ALIENATE HIMSELF FURTHER FROM THE JUDGE, THE JURY,
AND EVEN FROM HIS CLIENTS AND THEIR SUPPORTERS.

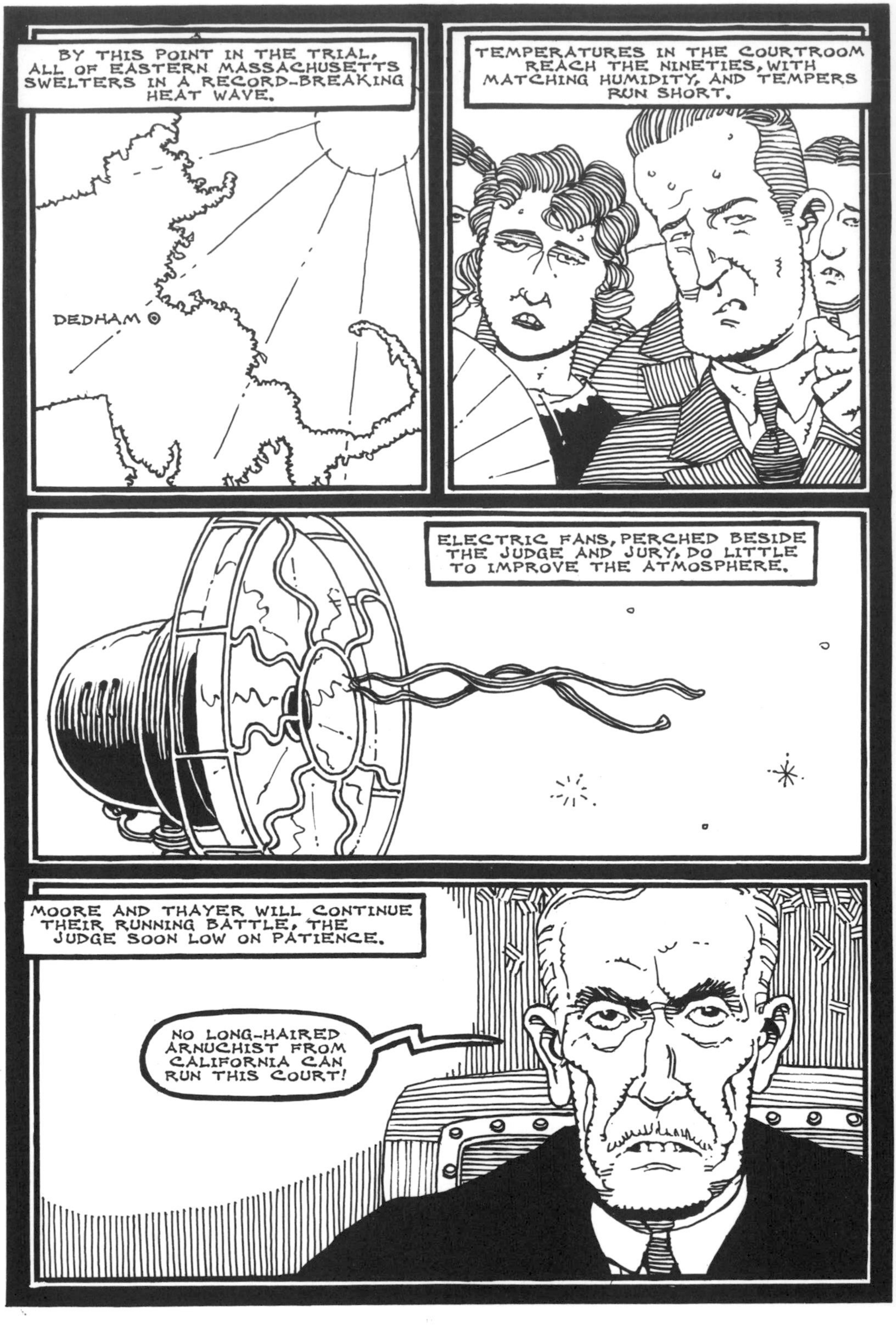
BY THIS POINT IN THE TRIAL, ALL OF EASTERN MASSACHUSETTS SWELTERS IN A RECORD-BREAKING HEAT WAVE.
DEDHAM
TEMPERATURES IN THE COURTROOM REACH THE NINETIES, WITH MATCHING HUMIDITY, AND TEMPERS RUN SHORT.
ELECTRIC FANS, PERCHED BESIDE THE JUDGE AND JURY, DO LITTLE TO IMPROVE THE ATMOSPHERE.
MOORE AND THAYER WILL CONTINUE THEIR RUNNING BATTLE, THE JUDGE SOON LOW ON PATIENCE.
NO LONG-HAIRED ARNUCHIST FROM CALIFORNIA CAN RUN THIS COURT!

MOORE BEGINS BY CALLING SIX CITIZENS FROM PLYMOUTH WHO RECALL HAVING SEEN VANZETTI SELLING FISH ON HIS USUAL ROUTE ON THE DAY OF THE SOUTH BRAINTREE MURDERS

ALL OF THEM ARE ITALIAN IMMIGRANTS WHO SPEAK ENGLISH HALTINGLY OR NEED THE AID OF AN INTERPRETER.

KATZMANN, IN HIS CROSS-EXAMINATION, SUCCEEDS IN CONFUSING THEM.

HOW CAN THEY BE CERTAIN OF WHAT THEY WERE DOING ON AN OTHERWISE UNREMARKABLE DAY OVER A YEAR AGO?

MOORE ALSO INTRODUCES 17 WITNESSES FROM THE CRIME SCENE

SEVERAL OF THEM STATE THAT THE TWO DEFENDANTS WERE NOT AMONG THE BANDITS WHILE OTHERS CAST DOUBT UPON THE PROSECUTION'S WITNESSES.

KATZMANN ASSAILS EACH OF THEM WITH A TORRENT OF MINUTE DETAIL, MAKING THEM APPEAR DOUBTFUL OR HESITANT.

HOW LONG DID YOU WATCH HIM?

I COULDN'T SAY.

GIVE US YOUR BEST JUDGEMENT.

IT WAS LESS THAN A MINUTE.

HOW MUCH LESS THAN A MINUTE?

I WOULDN'T KNOW.

MORE THAN HALF A MINUTE?

MOORE NEXT ATTEMPTS TO ESTABLISH SACCO'S ALIBI FOR THE DAY OF THE CRIME.

HIS CLIENT INSISTS THAT, ON APRIL 15, 1920, HE WAS IN BOSTON AT THE OFFICE OF THE ITALIAN CONSULATE...

TRYING TO OBTAIN TRAVEL PAPERS FOR A RETURN TO HIS HOMELAND.

HE PRESENTED A LARGE PHOTOGRAPH OF HIMSELF AND HIS FAMILY, UNUSABLE, HE WAS TOLD, FOR A PASSPORT.

UNFORTUNATELY, THE CLERK, GUISEPPI ANDROWER, HAS RETURNED TO ITALY.

IN ILL HEALTH, HE CANNOT TRAVEL TO AMERICA, BUT INSTEAD HAS SUBMITTED A DEPOSITION.

IN IT, ANDROWER REMEMBERS SHARING A LAUGH WITH HIS COLLEAGUES OVER THE MAN'S INAPPROPRIATE PHOTOGRAPH.

AND HE RECALLS TAKING NOTE OF THE DATE.

IN ADDITION, THREE MEN ARE CALLED TO THE STAND WHO REMEMBER HAVING DINED WITH SACCO AT BONI'S RESTAURANT IN BOSTON ON THE FATEFUL DAY.

KATZMANN CALLS THE VERACITY OF THESE WITNESSES INTO QUESTION:

AREN'T ALL THREE EITHER ITALIAN OR ANARCHIST OR BOTH?

MOORE NEXT PLANS TO INTRODUCE THOSE WHO WILL TESTIFY AS TO THE DEFENDANTS' OVERALL GOOD CHARACTER, THEIR HABITS OF HARD WORK AND LOYALTY, THEIR REPUTATIONS AS PEACEFUL AND LAW-ABIDING CITIZENS.

BUT FOR REASONS NEVER FULLY EXPLAINED, BOTH SIDES AGREE NOT TO PRESENT CHARACTER EVIDENCE EITHER POSITIVE OR NEGATIVE.

TUESDAY JUNE 28
THE FIREARMS CONTROVERSY RETURNS AS THE DEFENSE INTRODUCES ITS PAIR OF EXPERTS:

JAMES BURNS OF THE UNITED STATES CARTRIDGE COMPANY.

J. HENRY FITZGERALD OF THE COLT FIREARMS COMPANY.

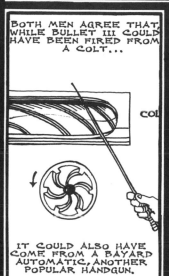

BOTH MEN AGREE THAT, WHILE BULLET III COULD HAVE BEEN FIRED FROM A COLT...

IT COULD ALSO HAVE COME FROM A BAYARD AUTOMATIC, ANOTHER POPULAR HANDGUN.

IN ANY CASE, THE FATAL BULLET WAS DEFINITELY NOT FIRED FROM SACCO'S AUTOMATIC.

THE TEST-FIRED BULLETS ARE NOT IN THE LEAST SIMILAR TO THE ONE IN QUESTION.

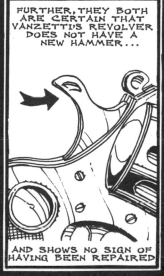

FURTHER, THEY BOTH ARE CERTAIN THAT VANZETTI'S REVOLVER DOES NOT HAVE A NEW HAMMER...

AND SHOWS NO SIGN OF HAVING BEEN REPAIRED

KATZMANN TRIES TO FLUSTER THEM WITH AN AVALANCHE OF DETAIL AND EVEN QUESTIONS THEIR PERSONAL FEELINGS ABOUT THE CASE.

BUT BOTH MEN HOLD THEIR GROUND.

TO MOST OBSERVERS THE BALLISTICS TESTIMONY HAS BEEN, "A CONFUSING WILDERNESS OF LANDS AND GROOVES."

IN THE END, THIS BATTLE OF EXPERTS APPARENTLY COMES TO A DRAW.

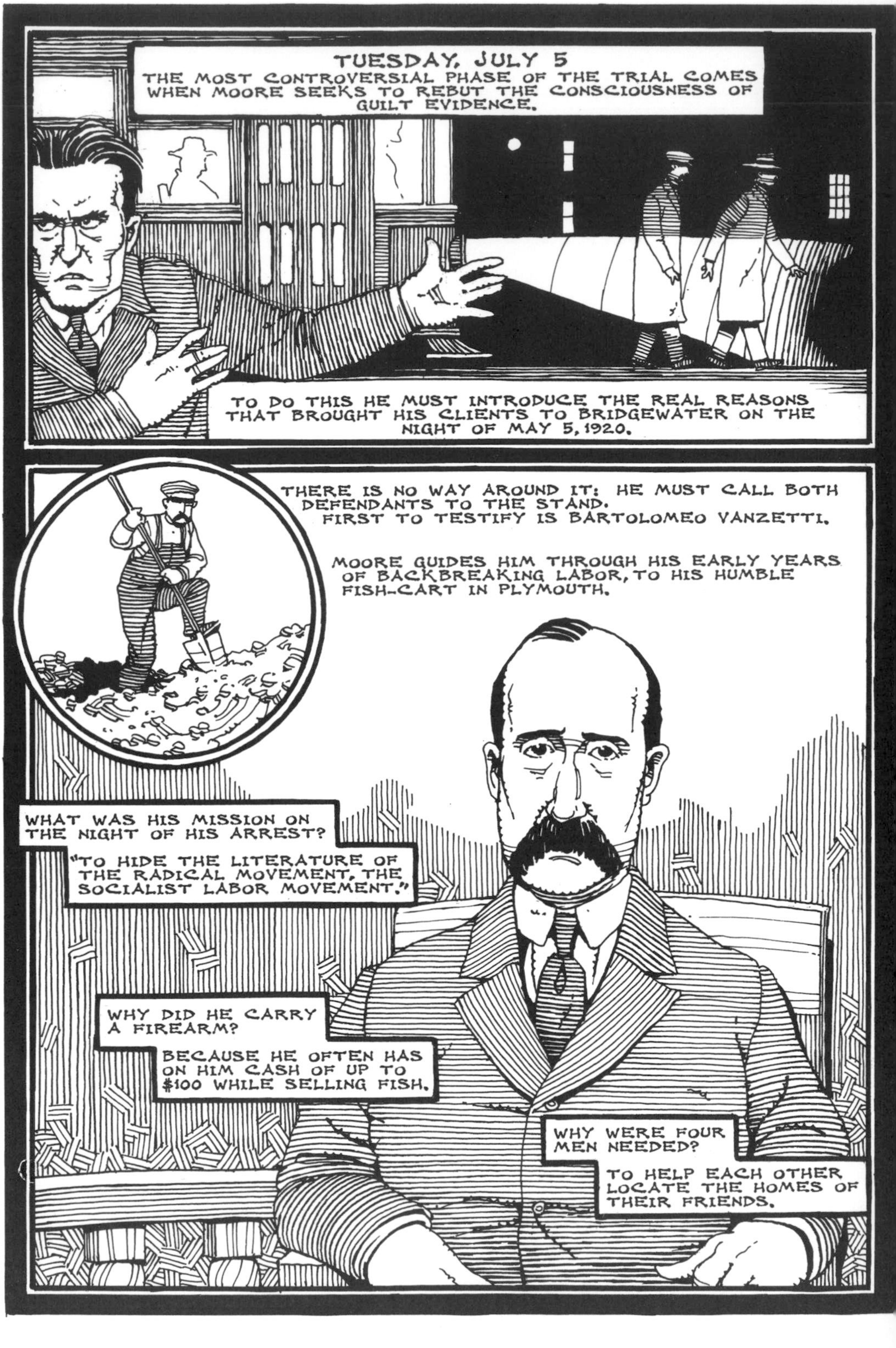
TUESDAY, JULY 5
THE MOST CONTROVERSIAL PHASE OF THE TRIAL COMES WHEN MOORE SEEKS TO REBUT THE CONSCIOUSNESS OF GUILT EVIDENCE.
TO DO THIS HE MUST INTRODUCE THE REAL REASONS THAT BROUGHT HIS CLIENTS TO BRIDGEWATER ON THE NIGHT OF MAY 5, 1920.
THERE IS NO WAY AROUND IT: HE MUST CALL BOTH DEFENDANTS TO THE STAND.
FIRST TO TESTIFY IS BARTOLOMEO VANZETTI.
MOORE GUIDES HIM THROUGH HIS EARLY YEARS OF BACKBREAKING LABOR, TO HIS HUMBLE FISH-CART IN PLYMOUTH.
WHAT WAS HIS MISSION ON THE NIGHT OF HIS ARREST?
"TO HIDE THE LITERATURE OF THE RADICAL MOVEMENT, THE SOCIALIST LABOR MOVEMENT."
WHY DID HE CARRY A FIREARM?
BECAUSE HE OFTEN HAS ON HIM CASH OF UP TO $100 WHILE SELLING FISH.
WHY WERE FOUR MEN NEEDED?
TO HELP EACH OTHER LOCATE THE HOMES OF THEIR FRIENDS.

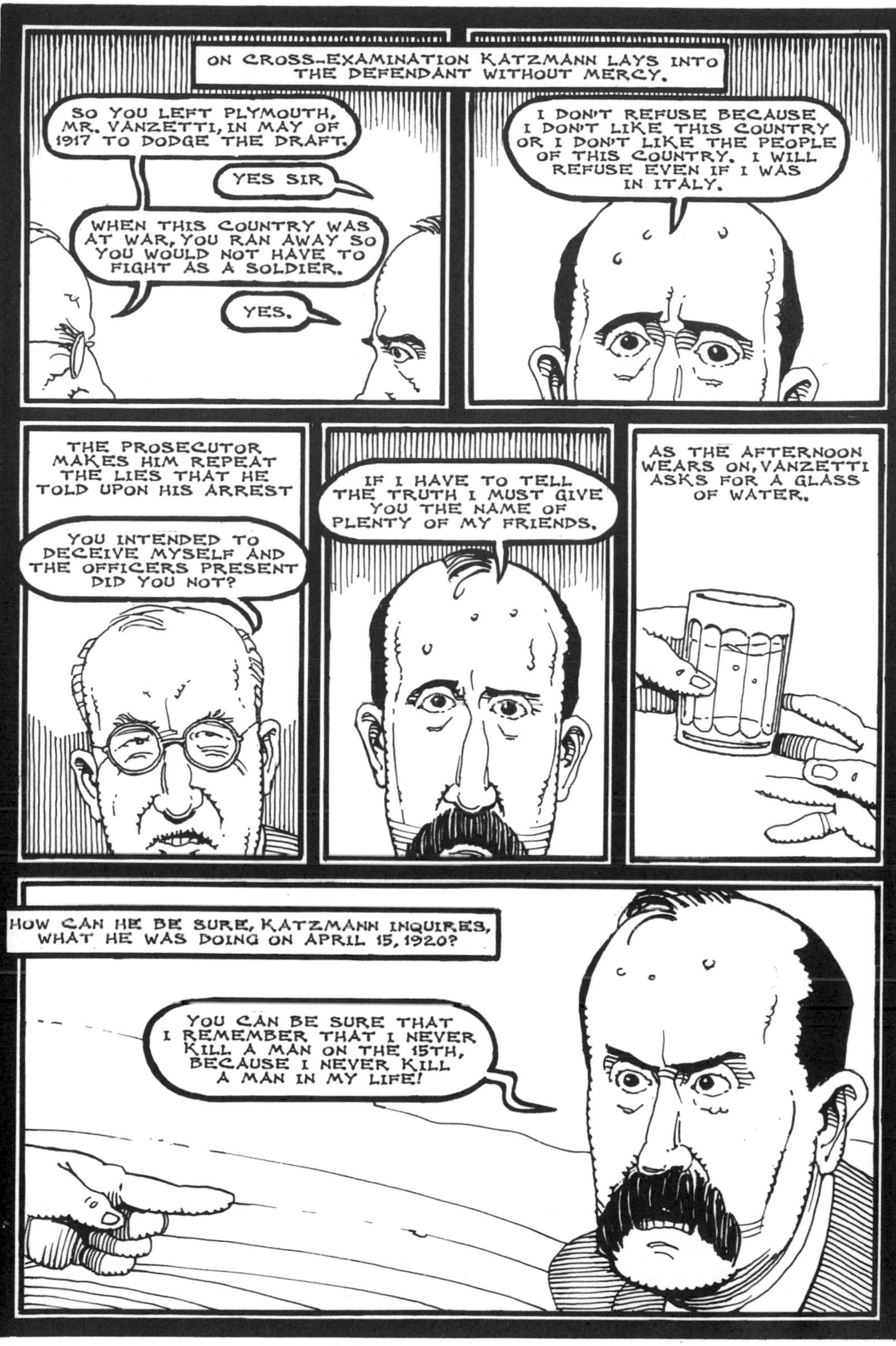
ON CROSS-EXAMINATION KATZMANN LAYS INTO THE DEFENDANT WITHOUT MERCY.
SO YOU LEFT PLYMOUTH, MR. VANZETTI, IN MAY OF 1917 TO DODGE THE DRAFT.
YES SIR
WHEN THIS COUNTRY WAS AT WAR, YOU RAN AWAY SO YOU WOULD NOT HAVE TO FIGHT AS A SOLDIER.
YES.
I DON'T REFUSE BECAUSE I DON'T LIKE THIS COUNTRY OR I DON'T LIKE THE PEOPLE OF THIS COUNTRY. I WILL REFUSE EVEN IF I WAS IN ITALY.
THE PROSECUTOR MAKES HIM REPEAT THE LIES THAT HE TOLD UPON HIS ARREST
YOU INTENDED TO DECEIVE MYSELF AND THE OFFICERS PRESENT DID YOU NOT?
IF I HAVE TO TELL THE TRUTH I MUST GIVE YOU THE NAME OF PLENTY OF MY FRIENDS.
AS THE AFTERNOON WEARS ON, VANZETTI ASKS FOR A GLASS OF WATER.
HOW CAN HE BE SURE, KATZMANN INQUIRES, WHAT HE WAS DOING ON APRIL 15, 1920?
YOU CAN BE SURE THAT I REMEMBER THAT I NEVER KILL A MAN ON THE 15TH, BECAUSE I NEVER KILL A MAN IN MY LIFE!

WEDNESDAY, JULY 6
NICOLA SACCO TAKES THE STAND.

HIS UNEASE IS APPARENT TO ALL.

AS HE DID WITH VANZETTI, MOORE LEADS HIM THROUGH HIS EARLY LIFE HIS MARRIAGE AND CHILDREN.

(ROSINA HAS BY THIS TIME GIVEN BIRTH TO A SECOND CHILD, INEZ.)

HIS SKILLED AND RESPONSIBLE JOB AT THE SHOE FACTORY...

HIS TRIP TO BOSTON ON THE DAY OF THE CRIME.

WHY DID HE COME TO AMERICA?

I WAS CRAZY TO COME TO THIS COUNTRY, BECAUSE I LIKED A FREE COUNTRY. CALL A FREE COUNTRY.

WHAT WHAS HIS MISSION ON THE NIGHT OF HIS ARREST?

IN NEW YORK THERE WAS SOMEBODY SAID THEY WERE TRYING TO ARREST ALL THE SOCIALISTS AND THE RADICALS, AND SO WE WERE ADVISED TO GO OVER TO THE FRIENDS TO GET THE BOOKS OUT AND GET NO TROUBLE. THE LITERATURE, I MEAN THE SOCIALIST LITERATURE.

AS A FINAL TOUCH MOORE HAS HIM TRY ON THE CAP RECOVERED FROM THE CRIME SCENE.

COULD NOT GO IN. MY SIZE IS 7 1/8.

IT IS OBVIOUSLY TOO SMALL AND PROMPTS LAUGHTER IN THE COURTROOM.

ON CROSS-EXAMINATION KATZMANN BEARS DOWN ON THE DEFENDANT WITH HIS USUAL FEROCITY.

DID YOU SAY YESTERDAY YOU LIVE A FREE COUNTRY?

YES SIR.

DID YOU LOVE THIS COUNTRY IN THE MONTH OF MAY 1917?

YES.

AND IN ORDER TO SHOW YOUR LOVE FOR THE UNITED STATES OF AMERICA, WHEN SHE WAS ABOUT TO CALL UPON YOU TO BECOME A SOLDIER, YOU RAN AWAY TO MEXICO!

WHENEVER MOORE OR ONE OF HIS ASSOCIATES OBJECTS TO A QUESTION THE JUDGE SNEERINGLY OVERRULES.

YOU OPENED UP THIS WHOLE SUBJECT.

I DON'T BELIEVE I OPENED IT UP.

ARE YOU GOING TO CLAIM THAT WHAT THE DEFENDANT DID—THIS COLLECTION OF BOOKS AND LITERATURE—WAS IN THE INTEREST OF THE UNITED STATES?

I NOW OBJECT TO YOUR HONOR'S STATEMENT AS PREJUDICIAL TO THE RIGHTS OF THE DEFENDANTS.

HIS COMPOSURE AND DIGNITY FINALLY IN TATTERS, SACCO IS ALLOWED TO GIVE A LENGTHY STATEMENT. HE CAN DO NAUGHT BUT FALL BACK ON HIS BELIEFS.

ANARCHISTIC IS NOT CRIMINALS!

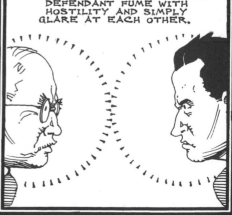

IN THE END, PROSECUTOR AND DEFENDANT FUME WITH HOSTILITY AND SIMPLY GLARE AT EACH OTHER.

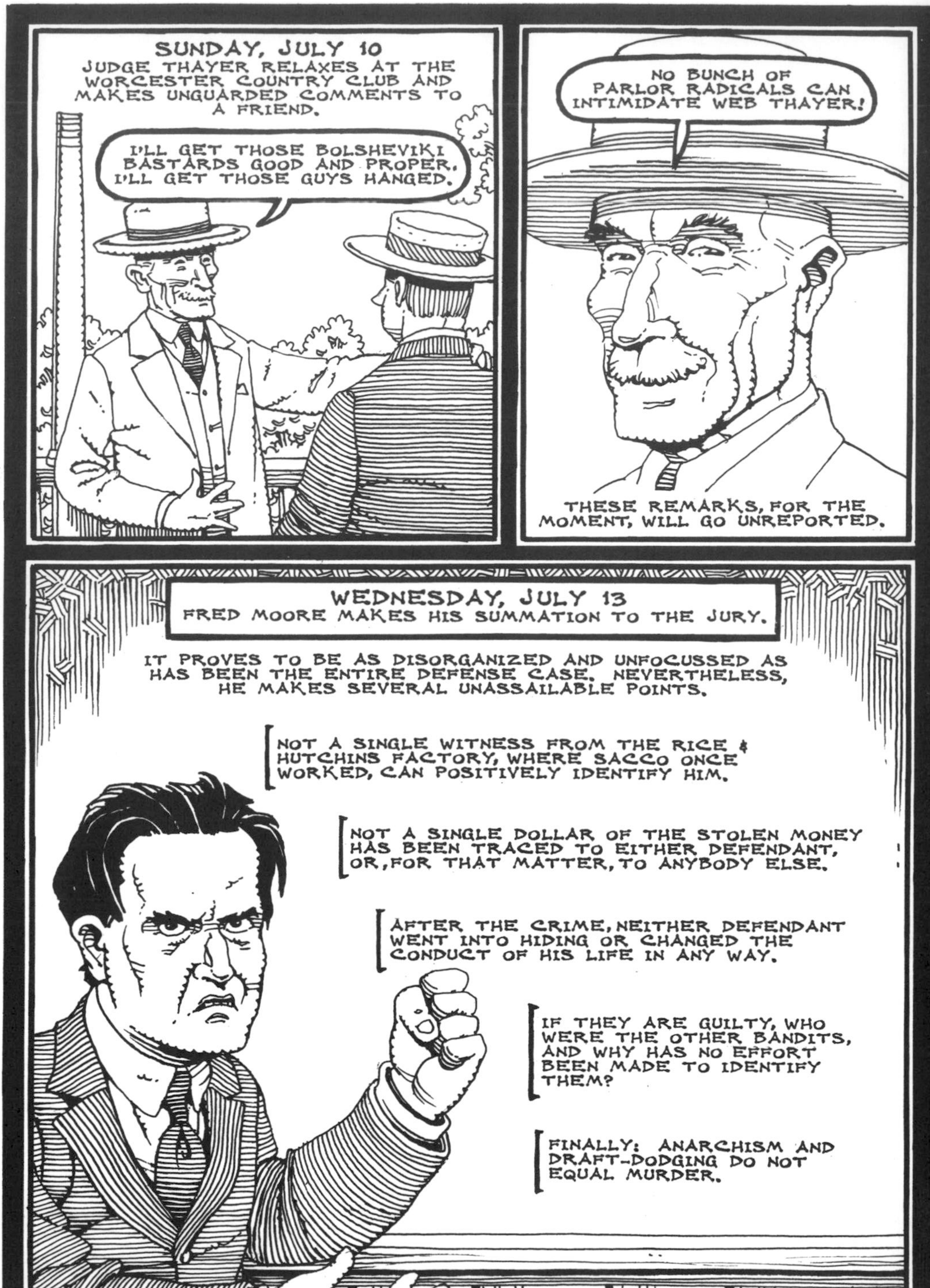

SUNDAY, JULY 10
JUDGE THAYER RELAXES AT THE WORCESTER COUNTRY CLUB AND MAKES UNGUARDED COMMENTS TO A FRIEND.
I'LL GET THOSE BOLSHEVIKI BASTARDS GOOD AND PROPER. I'LL GET THOSE GUYS HANGED.
NO BUNCH OF PARLOR RADICALS CAN INTIMIDATE WEB THAYER!
THESE REMARKS, FOR THE MOMENT, WILL GO UNREPORTED.
WEDNESDAY, JULY 13
FRED MOORE MAKES HIS SUMMATION TO THE JURY.
IT PROVES TO BE AS DISORGANIZED AND UNFOCUSSED AS HAS BEEN THE ENTIRE DEFENSE CASE. NEVERTHELESS, HE MAKES SEVERAL UNASSAILABLE POINTS.
NOT A SINGLE WITNESS FROM THE RICE & HUTCHINS FACTORY, WHERE SACCO ONCE WORKED, CAN POSITIVELY IDENTIFY HIM.
NOT A SINGLE DOLLAR OF THE STOLEN MONEY HAS BEEN TRACED TO EITHER DEFENDANT, OR, FOR THAT MATTER, TO ANYBODY ELSE.
AFTER THE CRIME, NEITHER DEFENDANT WENT INTO HIDING OR CHANGED THE CONDUCT OF HIS LIFE IN ANY WAY.
IF THEY ARE GUILTY, WHO WERE THE OTHER BANDITS, AND WHY HAS NO EFFORT BEEN MADE TO IDENTIFY THEM?
FINALLY: ANARCHISM AND DRAFT-DODGING DO NOT EQUAL MURDER.

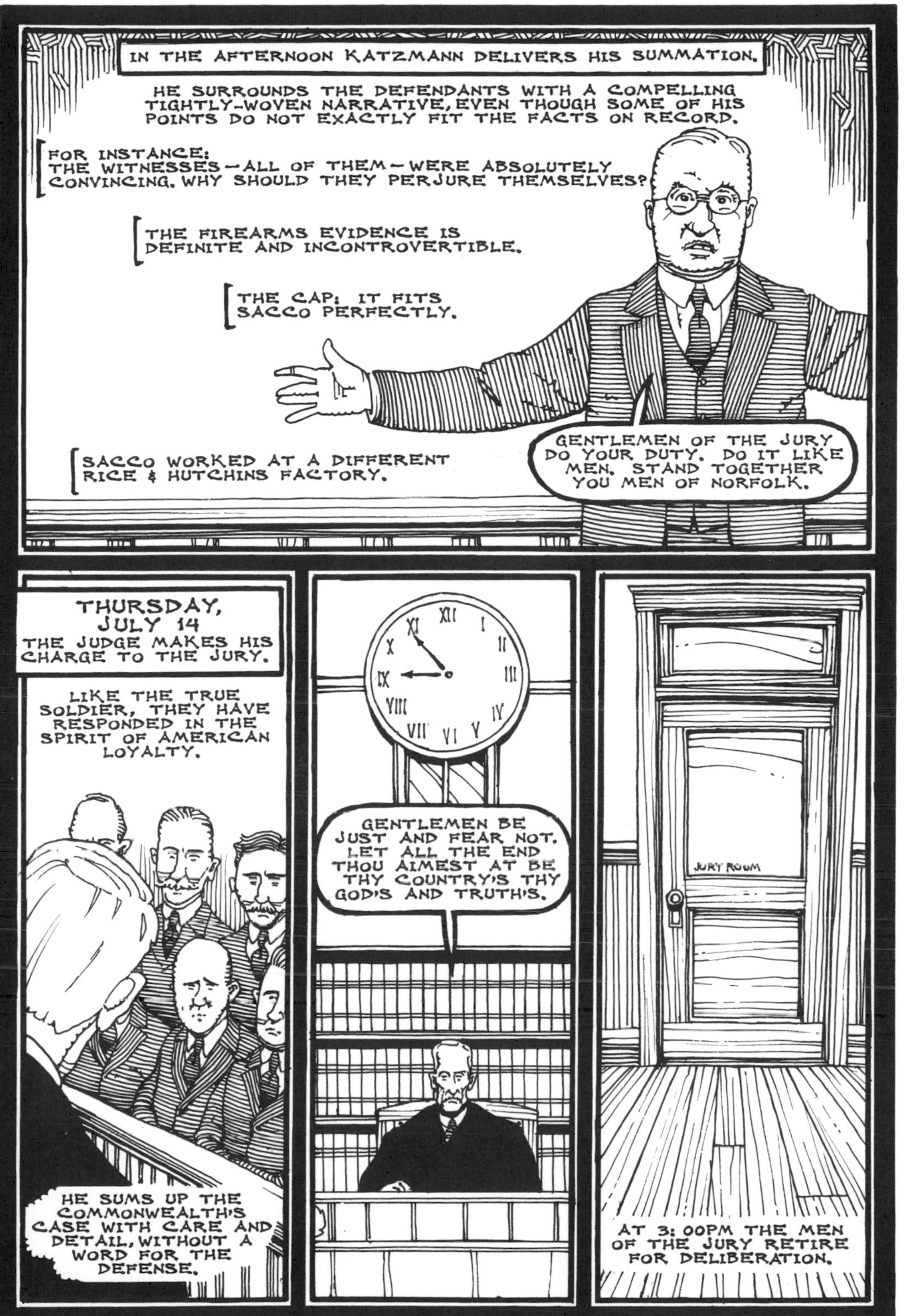
IN THE AFTERNOON KATZMANN DELIVERS HIS SUMMATION.
HE SURROUNDS THE DEFENDANTS WITH A COMPELLING TIGHTLY-WOVEN NARRATIVE, EVEN THOUGH SOME OF HIS POINTS DO NOT EXACTLY FIT THE FACTS ON RECORD.
FOR INSTANCE: THE WITNESSES—ALL OF THEM—WERE ABSOLUTELY CONVINCING. WHY SHOULD THEY PERJURE THEMSELVES?
THE FIREARMS EVIDENCE IS DEFINITE AND INCONTROVERTIBLE.
THE CAP: IT FITS SACCO PERFECTLY.
SACCO WORKED AT A DIFFERENT RICE & HUTCHINS FACTORY.
GENTLEMEN OF THE JURY DO YOUR DUTY. DO IT LIKE MEN. STAND TOGETHER YOU MEN OF NORFOLK.
THURSDAY, JULY 14 THE JUDGE MAKES HIS CHARGE TO THE JURY.
LIKE THE TRUE SOLDIER, THEY HAVE RESPONDED IN THE SPIRIT OF AMERICAN LOYALTY.
HE SUMS UP THE COMMONWEALTH'S CASE WITH CARE AND DETAIL, WITHOUT A WORD FOR THE DEFENSE.
GENTLEMEN BE JUST AND FEAR NOT. LET ALL THE END THOU AIMEST AT BE THY COUNTRY'S THY GOD'S AND TRUTH'S.
JURY ROOM
AT 3:00PM THE MEN OF THE JURY RETIRE FOR DELIBERATION.

INSIDE THE JURY ROOM (AS WILL BE LATER REVEALED) THE FIRST STRAW POLL COMES UP 10-2 FOR CONVICTION.

TO THEM THE BULLET EVIDENCE CARRIES MORE WEIGHT THAN DO THE EYEWITNESSES.

AN IMPORTANT FACT IS THAT THE SHELLS FROM THE CRIME SCENE MATCH THE ASSORTMENT FOUND IN SACCO'S POCKET (A POINT NOT MENTIONED IN THE COMMONWEALTH'S SUMMATION.)

NOBODY BRINGS UP THE SUBJECT OF THE DEFENDANTS' RADICALISM.

AT 8:00PM THE JURY EMERGES WITH ITS VERDICT:

NICOLA SACCO: GUILTY

BARTOLOMEO VANZETTI: GUILTY

IN THE FIRST DEGREE UPON EACH INDICTMENT.

AS THEY FILE OUT, SACCO RISES.

SONO INNOCENTE! YOU KILL TWO INNOCENT MEN!

HIS WIFE RUNS TO HIM.

WHAT AM I GOING TO DO? I'VE GOT TWO CHILDREN! OH, NICK! THEY KILL MY MAN!

PART V

THE LEGAL
JUNGLE

AFTER THE CONVICTIONS, SACCO REMAINS IN THE
DEDHAM JAIL, WHILE VANZETTI IS RETURNED TO THE
STATE PRISON IN CHARLESTOWN...

AND FRED MOORE INITIATES A SERIES OF APPEALS
ON THEIR BEHALF.

HIS FIRST APPEAL FILED JUST AFTER THE VERDCT IS ON THE GROUND THAT THE DECISION WENT AGAINST THE WEIGHT OF THE EVIDENCE.

HE THEN PROCEEDS WITH A SERIES OF SUPPLEMENTAL MOTIONS, BASED UPON NEWLY DISCOVERED EVIDENCE

TUESDAY, NOVEMBER 8, 1921
THE FIRST OF THEM, KNOWN AS THE "RIPLEY-DALEY"MOTION, IS BASED UPON THE ALLEGED MISCONDUCT OF WALTER RIPLEY, THE JURY FOREMAN (WHO HAS SINCE PASSED AWAY.)

GUILTY.

AS REPORTED BY HIS FRIEND WILLIAM DALEY.

IN THE DAYS BEFORE THE TRIAL, RIPLEY MENTIONED THAT HE MIGHT BE SELECTED FOR THE JURY IN THE SACCO-VANZETTI CASE.

WHEN DALEY OFFERED THE OPINION THAT THE TWO WERE PROBABLY NOT GUILTY, RIPLEY REPLIED:

DAMN THEM! THEY OUGHT TO HANG THEM ANYWAY!

SUCH UNACCEPTABLE BIAS SHOULD BE GROUNDS FOR A NEW TRIAL.

THURSDAY, MAY 4, 1922
THE SECOND SUPPLEMENTARY MOTION, CALLED "GOULD-PELSER," REFERS TO TWO EYEWITNESSES:

ROY GOULD WALKING ALONG PEARL ST. HAD A DIRECT VIEW OF THE SHOOTING AND WAS FIRED UPON FROM THE GETAWAY CAR.

HE GAVE HIS ADDRESS TO THE POLICE AND THEN LEFT TOWN, YET SOMEHOW HE WAS NEVER CALLED TO TESTIFY.

TRACKED DOWN IN CANADA HE STATES HIS CERTAINTY THAT SACCO WAS NOT THE GUNMAN.

LOUIS PELSER IS THE PROSECUTION WITNESS WHO SAW THE MURDERS FROM A WINDOW IN THE RICE & HUTCHINS FACTORY.

AND IDENTIFIED SACCO AS THE PERPETRATOR

HE NOW RECANTS THE STORY: HE CANNOT MAKE A POSITIVE IDENTIFICATION.

THE DISTRICT ATTORNEY'S MEN, HE SAYS "PERSUADED" HIM INTO HIS TESTIMONY.

SATURDAY, JULY 22, 1922
THE THIRD SUPPLEMENTARY MOTION IS PRESENTED: THE "GOODRIDGE" MOTION.

CARLOS GOODRIDGE, A MAJOR PROSECUTION WITNESS, WAS CERTAIN THAT SACCO WAS THE BANDIT FIRING FROM THE GETAWAY CAR.

NOW HIS TRUTHFULNESS IS IN TATTERS: HIS ACTUAL NAME IS ERASTUS WHITNEY.

AND HE HAS AN EXTENSIVE HISTORY AS FELON AND CON ARTIST.

MONDAY, SEPTEMBER 11, 1922
THE FOURTH SUPPLEMENTARY MOTION DEALS WITH ANOTHER KEY PROSECUTION WITNESS:

LOLA ANDREWS.

SHE CLAIMED AT THE TRIAL TO HAVE SEEN SACCO ON PEARL STREET, WORKING ON THE ENGINE OF THE BUICK.

BUT THOSE WHO KNOW THE WOMAN (WHOSE REAL NAME IS RACHEL HASSAM) SAY THAT SHE IS THOROUGHLY DISHONEST, UNRELIABLE AND UNSAVORY.

MOORE SOMEHOW PERSUADES HER TO SIGN AN AFFIDAVIT RECANTING HER IDENTIFICATION OF SACCO.

MONDAY, NOVEMBER 8, 1923
MOTION FIVE, THE "HAMILTON-PROCTOR" MOTION, ADDRESSES THE CRUCIAL FIREARMS EVIDENCE.

ALBERT HAMILTON IS A BALLISTICS EXPERT WHO HAS COMPARED BULLET III WITH THOSE FIRED FROM SACCO'S PISTOL...

USING THE POWERFUL BAUSCH & LOMB COMPOUND MICROSCOPE STRONGER THAN ANY AVAILABLE TO THE EXPERTS AT THE TRIAL.

HE DECLARES THAT THE BULLET IN QUESTION DID NOT COME FROM SACCO'S AUTOMATIC.

CAPT. WILLIAM PROCTOR, THE PROSECUTION EXPERT, NOW WISHES TO CLARIFY HIS ORIGINAL TESTIMONY.

HE FEELS THAT HE MISLED THE JURY BY SAYING THAT BULLET III WAS "CONSISTENT WITH" SACCO'S COLT

HE DID NOT MEAN TO SUGGEST THAT THERE WAS A DEFINITE MATCH

(ALTHOUGH IT WAS DESCRIBED AS SUCH BY THE COMMONWEALTH.)

DURING THE YEARS THAT MOORE SPENDS PREPARING AND FILING HIS APPEALS, SACCO AND VANZETTI LANGUISH IN THEIR SEPARATE PRISONS...

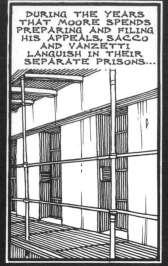

AS FRIENDS AND SUPPORTERS SEND OUT COUNTLESS LETTERS OF APPEAL FOR FINANCIAL ASSISTANCE.

A CAMPAIGN, TO THIS POINT, UNSUCCESSFUL.

INTEREST IS HIGHER, HOWEVER, OUTSIDE THE UNITED STATES.

DEMONSTRATIONS ARE STAGED THROUGHOUT LATIN AMERICA: CUBA, PANAMA, BRAZIL, CHILE, AND MEXICO.

IN EUROPE, THREATS ARE RECEIVED BY AMERICAN DIPLOMATS.

A BOMB EXPLODES AT THE HOME OF THE U.S. AMBASSADOR TO FRANCE (ONE EMPLOYEE INJURED).

MONDAY, OCTOBER 1, 1923
A HEARING OPENS IN WHICH THE FIVE SUPPLEMENTARY MOTIONS ARE ARGUED BY MOORE AND KATZMANN BEFORE JUDGE THAYER.

A PECULIARITY OF THE LAW IN MASSACHUSETTS AT THIS TIME REQUIRES THAT THE JUDGE WHO PRESIDED OVER THE ORIGINAL TRIAL HEAR ALL APPEALS...

THUS ASKING THAYER TO RULE AGAINST HIMSELF.

THE FIRST THING MOORE DISCOVERS IS THAT PELSER AND ANDREWS, THE TWO WITNESSES WHO RECANTED, HAVE NOW RETRACTED THEIR RECANTATIONS...

(APPARENTLY AFTER FURTHER "PERSUASION" BY KATZMANN).

ANOTHER SURPRISE COMES IN NOVEMBER, WHEN MOORE INTRODUCES HIS FIREARMS EXPERTS.

OPPOSING HIM IS THE NEW DISTRICT ATTORNEY, HAROLD WILLIAMS, WHO IS LEFT WITH HIS ONLY EXPERT CAPTAIN VAN AMBURGH.

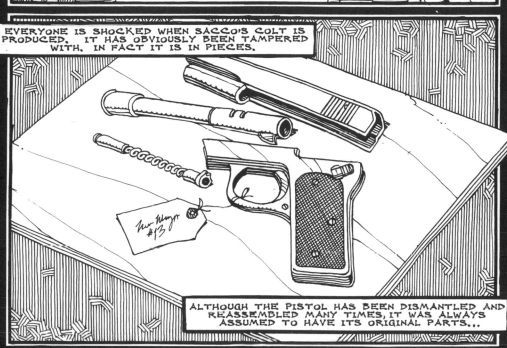

EVERYONE IS SHOCKED WHEN SACCO'S COLT IS PRODUCED. IT HAS OBVIOUSLY BEEN TAMPERED WITH. IN FACT IT IS IN PIECES.

ALTHOUGH THE PISTOL HAS BEEN DISMANTLED AND REASSEMBLED MANY TIMES, IT WAS ALWAYS ASSUMED TO HAVE ITS ORIGINAL PARTS...

BUT THE DEFENSE EXPERT HAMILTON NOTICES THAT THE BARREL IS NOW WIDER THAN BEFORE.

THE ORIGINAL BARREL WAS APPARENTLY REMOVED AND ATTACHED TO ANOTHER PISTOL FOR THE RECENT ROUND OF TEST FIRINGS.

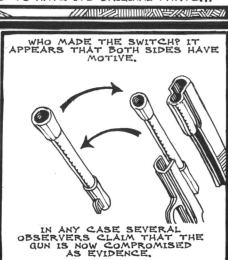

WHO MADE THE SWITCH? IT APPEARS THAT BOTH SIDES HAVE MOTIVE.

IN ANY CASE SEVERAL OBSERVERS CLAIM THAT THE GUN IS NOW COMPROMISED AS EVIDENCE.

AS THE APPEALS PROCESS DRAGS ON, SACCO KEENLY FEELS THE PRESSURE OF HIS INCARCERATION.

AFTER VISITS BY HIS WIFE AND CHILDREN, HE DESCENDS INTO PROLONGED DEPRESSION.

IN MARCH OF 1923, AFTER AN ATTEMPT TO STARVE HIMSELF, HE IS ORDERED TO UNDERGO EXAMINATION BY A TEAM OF ALIENISTS...

AFTER WHICH HE IS REMOVED TO THE BOSTON PSYCHIATRIC HOSPITAL FOR A FULL EVALUATION.

THE JUDGE AND DISTRICT ATTORNEY ASSUME THAT HE IS FAKING...

BUT THE DOCTORS BELIEVE OTHERWISE, AND HE IS COMMITTED TO THE STATE MENTAL HOSPITAL IN BRIDGEWATER.

FRIDAY, SEPTEMBER 28, 1923
AFTER A FIVE-MONTH STAY, SACCO IS DEEMED READY FOR RELEASE AND IS RETURNED TO HIS CELL IN DEDHAM.

VANZETTI, IN THE MEANTIME, IS SUSTAINED BY AN INNATE RESILIENCE.

HE ACCEPTS HIS FATE AS A VICTIM OF CLASS WARFARE.

IN HIS CELL, HE READS VORACIOUSLY.

HE EXCHANGES CORRESPONDENCE WITH A LARGE GROUP OF WELL-WISHERS AND SUPPORTERS...

ALL OF WHOM MARVEL AT THE ARTICULATE AND EXPRESSIVE FLUENCY OF HIS WRITING.

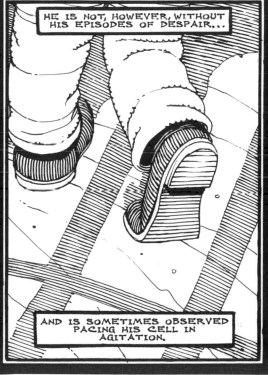

HE IS NOT, HOWEVER, WITHOUT HIS EPISODES OF DESPAIR...

AND IS SOMETIMES OBSERVED PACING HIS CELL IN AGITATION.

THE SACCO-VANZETTI DEFENSE COMMITTEE CONTINUES TO STRUGGLE DURING THESE YEARS WHEN THE CASE IS OUT OF THE PUBLIC EYE.

ALDINO FELICANI, TIRELESS IN HIS LOYALTY, WORKS TO BALANCE THE COMPETING INTERESTS OF VARIOUS LEFTIST FACTIONS.

ALSO OF INVALUABLE AID ARE SEVERAL BOSTON WOMEN, OF REPUTABLE FAMILIES AND LIBERAL LEANINGS, WHO WORK FOR PRISON REFORM AND SOCIAL CHANGE.

CHIEF AMONG THEM IS MRS. ELIZABETH GLENDOWER EVANS (KNOWN AS "AUNTIE BEE"), WHO ATTENDED NEARLY EVERY DAY OF THE TRIAL.

SHE AND HER COHORTS WRITE LETTERS AND ARTICLES AND CIRCULATE PETITIONS FOR THE PRISONERS.

ONE LADY, VIRGINIA MACMECHAM, TEACHES VANZETTI ENGLISH IN HIS CELL.

OTHERS HAVE BEFRIENDED ROSINA SACCO AND HER CHILDREN...

DRIVING THEM ON ERRANDS PROVIDING THEM WITH FOOD AND COMFORT.

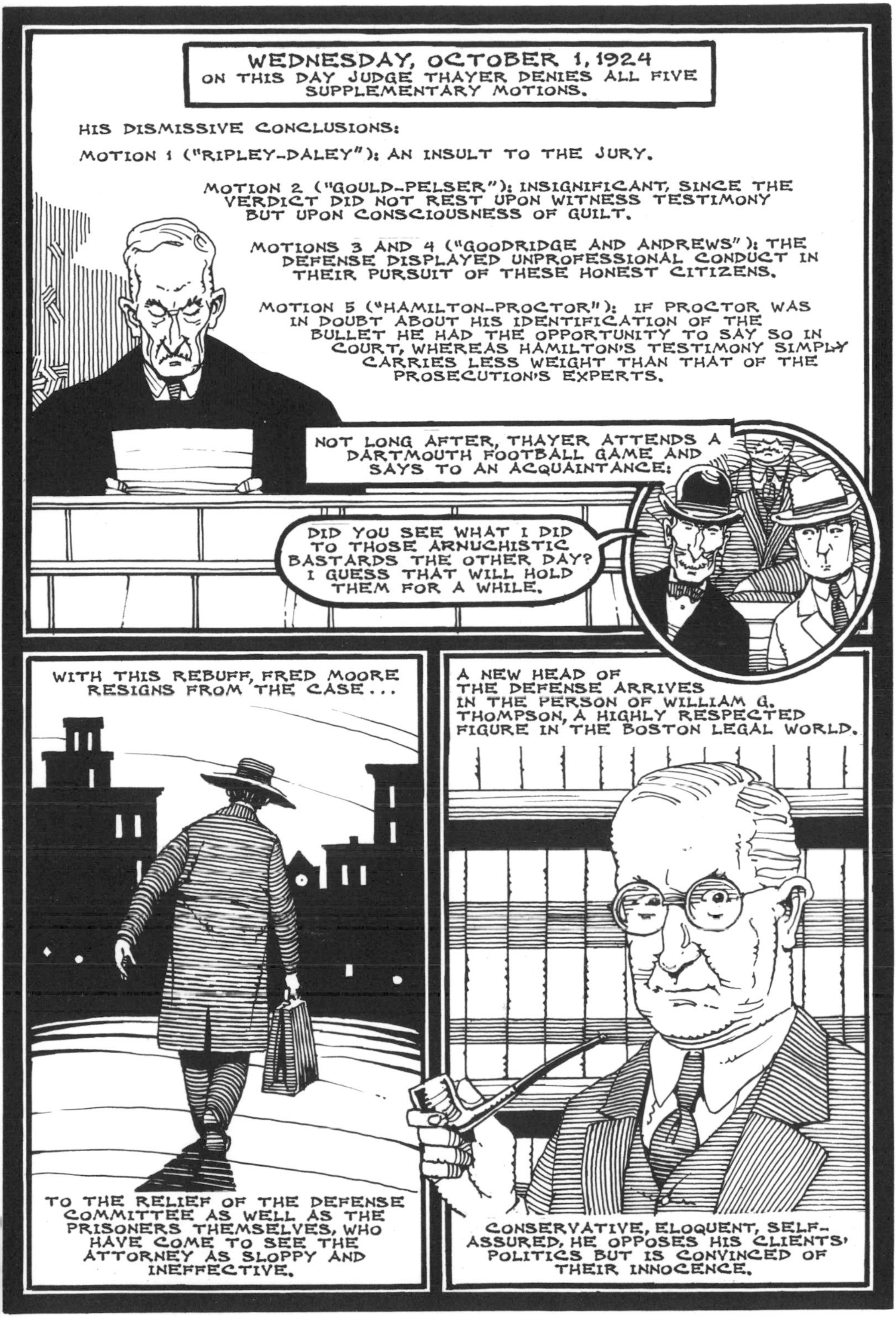
WEDNESDAY, OCTOBER 1, 1924
ON THIS DAY JUDGE THAYER DENIES ALL FIVE SUPPLEMENTARY MOTIONS.
HIS DISMISSIVE CONCLUSIONS:
MOTION 1 ("RIPLEY-DALEY"): AN INSULT TO THE JURY.
MOTION 2 ("GOULD-PELSER"): INSIGNIFICANT, SINCE THE VERDICT DID NOT REST UPON WITNESS TESTIMONY BUT UPON CONSCIOUSNESS OF GUILT.
MOTIONS 3 AND 4 ("GOODRIDGE AND ANDREWS"): THE DEFENSE DISPLAYED UNPROFESSIONAL CONDUCT IN THEIR PURSUIT OF THESE HONEST CITIZENS.
MOTION 5 ("HAMILTON-PROCTOR"): IF PROCTOR WAS IN DOUBT ABOUT HIS IDENTIFICATION OF THE BULLET HE HAD THE OPPORTUNITY TO SAY SO IN COURT, WHEREAS HAMILTON'S TESTIMONY SIMPLY CARRIES LESS WEIGHT THAN THAT OF THE PROSECUTION'S EXPERTS.
NOT LONG AFTER, THAYER ATTENDS A DARTMOUTH FOOTBALL GAME AND SAYS TO AN ACQUAINTANCE:
DID YOU SEE WHAT I DID TO THOSE ARNUCHISTIC BASTARDS THE OTHER DAY? I GUESS THAT WILL HOLD THEM FOR A WHILE.
WITH THIS REBUFF, FRED MOORE RESIGNS FROM THE CASE...
TO THE RELIEF OF THE DEFENSE COMMITTEE AS WELL AS THE PRISONERS THEMSELVES, WHO HAVE COME TO SEE THE ATTORNEY AS SLOPPY AND INEFFECTIVE.
A NEW HEAD OF THE DEFENSE ARRIVES IN THE PERSON OF WILLIAM G. THOMPSON, A HIGHLY RESPECTED FIGURE IN THE BOSTON LEGAL WORLD.
CONSERVATIVE, ELOQUENT, SELF-ASSURED, HE OPPOSES HIS CLIENTS' POLITICS BUT IS CONVINCED OF THEIR INNOCENCE.

A NEW HOPE ARISES IN NOVEMBER OF 1925, WHEN SACCO IS SLIPPED A NOTE FROM ANOTHER PRISONER IN THE NORFOLK COUNTY JAIL.

THE PRISONER IS CELESTINO MADIEROS, A CONVICTED MURDERER HIMSELF, WHO OFFERS A REMARKABLE CONFESSION:

HE WAS PART OF THE GANG THAT COMMITTED THE MURDERS IN SOUTH BRAINTREE, AND SACCO AND VANZETTI WERE NOT AMONG THEM.

ON THE MORNING OF APRIL 15, 1920, HE SAYS, HE WAS PICKED UP IN PROVIDENCE BY FOUR MEN IN A HUDSON.

THEY LEFT THE HUDSON IN THE WOODS AND CLIMBED INTO A BUICK WITH CURTAINED WINDOWS AND DROVE ON TO THE CRIME.

THE MEN WERE OBVIOUSLY PROFESSIONAL CRIMINALS AND BOASTED OF THEIR PREVIOUS JOBS ROBBING FREIGHT CARS.

MADIEROS CARRIED A .38 COLT AUTOMATIC BUT DID NOT USE IT.

HE CAME AWAY WITH $2800 IN CASH, A FIFTH SHARE OF THE PAYROLL MONEY.

HE REFUSES, HOWEVER, TO NAME HIS COMPANIONS, AND SEVERAL OF HIS MEMORIES DO NOT FIT THE FACTS.

FOR INSTANCE, HE CLAIMS THAT THE PAYROLL CASH WAS IN A SINGLE BLACK BAG.

A LITTLE INVESTIGATION BY THE DEFENSE TEAM UNCOVERS THE PROBABLE CULPRITS:

A GANG BASED IN PROVIDENCE LED BY ONE JOE MORELLI.

THEY ARE KNOWN TO SPECIALIZE IN RAIL SHIPMENTS TO SHOE FACTORIES.

HIS RESEMBLANCE TO NICOLA SACCO IS MARKED BY MANY.

THE GROUP CONSISTED, AT VARIOUS TIMES, OF JOE'S BROTHERS MIKE, PATSY, BUTSY, AND FRED

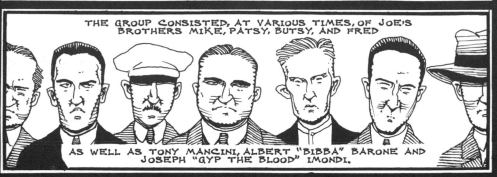

AS WELL AS TONY MANCINI, ALBERT "BIBBA" BARONE AND JOSEPH "GYP THE BLOOD" IMONDI.

ANOTHER MEMBER WAS STEVE "THE POLE" BENKOSKI...

WHO COULD HAVE BEEN THE PALE BLONDE MAN DESCRIBED BY WITNESSES.

THESE MEN ARE LIFELONG THIEVES OF THE MOST HARDENED VARIETY.

WORD IS THAT, AT THE TIME, THEY WERE IN NEED OF CASH TO FINANCE THEIR DEFENSE IN ANOTHER CASE.

JOE MORELLI, CURRENTLY IMPRISONED FOR ANOTHER MURDER, EXPECTEDLY DENIES ALL INVOLVEMENT.

MONDAY, JANUARY 11, 1926
THE CASE OF THE COMMONWEALTH V. SACCO AND VANZETTI IS ARGUED BEFORE THE FIVE-MEMBER MASSACHUSETTS SUPREME JUDICIAL COURT.

WILLIAM THOMPSON CONFRONTS THE ASSISTANT DISTRICT ATTORNEY DUDLEY RANNEY.

THE COURT, HOWEVER, CANNOT RULE UPON EVIDENCE OF GUILT OR INNOCENCE BUT ONLY UPON MATTERS OF LAW AND JUDICIAL CONDUCT.

AND IN THIS THE JUSTICES ULTIMATELY DECIDE TO BREAK NO NEW GROUND.

WEDNESDAY, MAY 12
THE COURT ANNOUNCES THAT IT UPHOLDS THE CONVICTIONS AND DENIES THE MOTION FOR A NEW TRIAL. THEY SEE NO REASON TO REVERSE JUDGE THAYER.

WEDNESDAY, MAY 26
UNDAUNTED, THOMPSON ARGUES A NEW SUPPLEMENTARY MOTION BEFORE THAYER, BASED UPON THE CONFESSION OF CELESTINO MADIEROS.

SATURDAY, OCTOBER 23
THAYER DENIES THIS MOTION. HE GRANTS MADIEROS - "A ROBBER, LIAR, CROOK AND THIEF" - NO CREDIBILITY WHATSOEVER.

AT THE DAWN OF THE NEW YEAR, TIME IS RUNNING OUT, AND FEW OPTIONS REMAIN AVAILABLE FOR THE TWO PRISONERS.

THURSDAY, JANUARY 27, 1927
ONE MORE APPEAL IS ARGUED BY WILLIAM THOMPSON BEFORE THE SUPREME JUDICIAL COURT, THIS ONE BASED UPON THE MADIEROS CONFESSION.

THE DEFENSE COMMITTEE RAMPS UP ITS EFFORTS WITH TWO NEW LEADERS:

THE ENERGETIC IRISH SOCIALIST MARY DONOVAN WHO INITIATES LETTER-WRITING CAMPAIGNS AND LEADS PUBLIC DEMONSTRATIONS...

AND THE JOURNALIST GARDNER JACKSON, WHO MANAGES PUBLICITY FOR THE RECHARGED EFFORT.

BUT THE CASE STUBBORNLY REMAINS A LOCAL MASSACHUSETTS ISSUE, UNTIL AN ARTICLE APPEARS IN THE MARCH ISSUE OF THE ATLANTIC MONTHLY, BY THE HARVARD PROFESSOR (AND FUTURE SUPREME COURT JUSTICE) FELIX FRANKFURTER.

HE CITES SEVERAL INSTANCES OF REVERSIBLE ERROR:

THE IDENTIFICATION OF SUSPECTS WITHOUT A POLICE LINEUP.

THE LATE-NIGHT ROUNDUP OF JURORS.

THE PROSECUTION'S CONCEALMENT OF THE EXONERATING WITNESS GOULD.

THE RED SCARE PREJUDICE AND ARMED GUARDS IN THE COURTHOUSE.

THE RETRACTION BY CAPT. WILLIAM PROCTOR.

JUDGE THAYER'S SNEERING COMMENTS REGARDING SACCO'S PATRIOTISM.

THE PREJUDICIAL STATEMENT BY JURY FOREMAN RIPLEY.

THE STOLEN MONEY — NEVER RECOVERED.

ALMOST OVERNIGHT THE ENTIRE COUNTRY IS TALKING ABOUT THE SACCO-VANZETTI CASE.

THE ATLANTIC MONTHLY

THURSDAY, APRIL 7
THE SUPREME JUDICIAL COURT DENIES THE MADIEROS MOTION. THE DEFENSE IS NOW AT THE END OF ITS LEGAL ROAD.

SATURDAY, APRIL 9
THE PRISONERS ARE BROUGHT BEFORE JUDGE THAYER ONE MORE TIME TO HEAR HIM PRONOUNCE SENTENCE.

HE COMMANDS THAT THEY:

SUFFER THE PUNISHMENT OF DEATH BY THE PASSAGE OF A CURRENT OF ELECTRICITY THROUGH YOUR BODY.

THE CONDEMNED ARE ALLOWED TO GIVE STATEMENTS:

I NEVER KNOW NEVER HEARD EVEN READ IN HISTORY ANYTHING SO CRUEL AS THIS COURT.

IN ALL MY LIFE I HAVE NEVER STOLE I HAVE NEVER KILLED AND I HAVE NEVER SPILLED BLOOD. YOU SEE BEFORE YOU NOT TREMBLING. YOU SEE ME LOOKING IN YOUR EYES STRAIGHT NOT BLUSHING NOT CHANGING COLOR NOT ASHAMED OR IN FEAR.

PART VI

A GLOBAL CAUSE

WITH RECOURSE TO THE COURT SYSTEM NOW AT AN END,
ALL EYES LOOK TO THE MASSACHUSETTS STATE HOUSE.

THE ONLY CHANCE FOR THE PRISONERS IS A
DECLARATION OF EXECUTIVE CLEMENCY FROM THE
GOVERNOR, ALVAN T. FULLER.

THE DEATH SENTENCES SET OFF A NEW ROUND OF RIOTS AND PROTESTS WORLDWIDE.

JUSTICE FOR

FRANCE TO PARAGUAY, IRELAND TO NEW ZEALAND.

ARTICLES AND EDITORIALS DECRY THE JUDGE'S DECISION.

OBSERVERS ACROSS THE POLITICAL SPECTRUM NOW BELIEVE THAT THE TRIAL WAS UNFAIR.

ALTHOUGH THE PUBLIC ATMOSPHERE TODAY IS MUCH IMPROVED FROM THE TIME OF THE RED SCARE...

GO HOME

OLD ANTIPATHIES TOWARD ITALIANS AND IMMIGRANTS REMAIN ALIVE AND ARE STIRRED UP ANEW.

H. G. WELLS

CLARENCE DARROW

ALBERT EINSTEIN

DOROTHY PARKER

WILLIAM ALLEN WHITE

WELL-KNOWN PERSONS FROM THE ARTS, SCIENCE, AND THE LAW COME FORWARD IN SUPPORT OF THE CONDEMNED MEN.

UPTON SINCLAIR

EDNA ST. VINCENT MILLAY

JOHN DOS PASSOS

H. L. MENCKEN

GEORGE BERNARD SHAW

THURSDAY, JUNE 2
PUBLIC PRESSURE COMPELS GOVERNOR FULLER TO ANNOUNCE THE FORMATION OF A SPECIAL COMMITTEE TO REVIEW THE EVIDENCE AND CONDUCT OF THE CASE.

THE PANEL CONSISTS OF THREE OF BOSTON'S MOST RESPECTED CITIZENS:

ABBOTT LAWRENCE LOWELL PRESIDENT OF HARVARD UNIVERSITY...

SAMUEL W. STRATTON PRESIDENT OF M. I. T...

AND RETIRED PROBATE JUDGE ROBERT GRANT.

IN CLOSED CHAMBERS, TO WHICH THE PUBLIC IS DENIED, THEY INTERVIEW THE PRINCIPAL FIGURES FROM THE TRIAL...

INCLUDING JUDGE THAYER, PROSECUTOR KATZMANN, AND ALL OF THE REMAINING JURORS.

THEY VISIT THE SCENE OF THE CRIME.

NO REPRESENTATIVES OF THE DEFENSE ARE ALLOWED INTO THE PROCEEDINGS.

BY THIS TIME, WILLIAM THOMPSON HAS RETIRED FROM THE CASE. HERBERT EHRMAN AND ARTHUR HILL NOW GUIDE WHAT IS LEFT OF THE EFFORT.

WEDNESDAY, AUGUST 3 THE COMMITTEE ANNOUNCES ITS DECISION:

IN SUPPORT OF THE VERDICT AGAINST SACCO AND VANZETTI.

MANY CYNICS ARE NOT SURPRISED.

THE COMMITTEE'S PURPOSE, THEY ASSUME, WAS NOT TO HONESTLY REVIEW THE CASE, BUT TO MAKE RESPECTABLE THAYER AND THE CONDUCT OF THE TRIAL.

VANZETTI, FOR ONE, BELIEVES THAT THE MACHINERY HAS BEEN IN MOTION FOR QUITE SOME TIME...

AND NOTHING CAN STOP IT.

DESPITE HUNDREDS OF LETTERS AND A PETITION SIGNED BY 475,000 CITIZENS, GOVERNOR FULLER DECLINES TO ISSUE A PARDON.

THE PRISONERS WILL DIE.

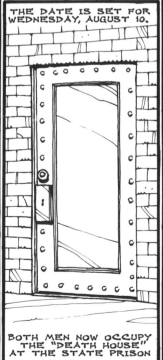

THE DATE IS SET FOR WEDNESDAY, AUGUST 10.

BOTH MEN NOW OCCUPY THE "DEATH HOUSE" AT THE STATE PRISON

SATURDAY, AUGUST 6 A FINAL DESPERATE MOTION IS ARGUED BEFORE THAYER, BASED UPON THE BIAS OF THE TRIAL JUDGE (THAYER).

TWO DAYS LATER, TO NO ONE'S SURPRISE, HE DENIES THIS APPEAL.

GOVERNOR FULLER STAYS THE EXECUTIONS, WHILE A LAST-MINUTE ATTEMPT IS MADE TO BRING THE CASE TO THE U.S. SUPREME COURT.

THOMPSON AND HILL VISIT JUSTICE OLIVER WENDELL HOLMES AT HIS VACATION HOME NORTH OF BOSTON.

THE VENERABLE JURIST OFFERS THEM LITTLE HOPE. IT IS NOT A MATTER FOR THE FEDERAL COURTS.

WE PRACTICE LAW, NOT JUSTICE.

THE EXECUTIONS ARE RESCHEDULED FOR AUGUST 22.

TUESDAY, AUGUST 9
THE RESULTS ARE ANNOUNCED OF NEW BALLISTICS TESTS, CONDUCTED BY MAJOR CALVIN GODDARD, USING THE NEWLY-DEVELOPED COMPARISON MICROSCOPE, WITH WHICH THE MARKINGS ON TWO BULLETS CAN BE VIEWED SIDE-BY-SIDE.

HIS CONCLUSION IS THAT BULLET III CAME FROM SACCO'S GUN.

SUPPORTERS OF THE CONDEMNED MEN DISPUTE THIS FINDING ON SEVERAL GROUNDS:

- THE COLT AUTOMATIC HAS BEEN SO ALTERED AND TEMPERED-WITH THAT IT IS NOW WORTHLESS AS EVIDENCE.

- THE BULLETS AND SHELLS IN QUESTION HAVE BEEN IN THE POSSESSION OF THE PROSECUTION EXPERT CAPT. CHARLES VAN AMBURGH.

- MAJOR GODDARD PREVIOUSLY DECLARED THAT HE ASSUMED SACCO TO BE GUILTY.

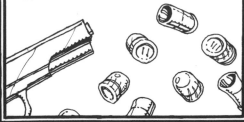

A MORE NEFARIOUS PROSPECT ARISES: WAS THE ORIGINAL BULLET SWITCHED AT SOME POINT IN THE PROCESS?

- WHY IS BULLET III DIFFERENT FROM THE OTHERS?

- DID NOT WITNESSES AT THE SCENE DESCRIBE A SINGLE GUNMAN FIRING INTO THE BODY OF BERARDELLI?

- DID NOT THE CORONER McGRATH AT THE INITIAL INQUEST STATE HIS BELIEF THAT ALL SIX BULLETS CAME FROM THE SAME GUN?

TUESDAY, AUGUST 16

THE HOME, IN EAST MILTON MASS., OF DEDHAM JUROR LEWIS McHARDY IS BOMBED.

THERE ARE NO INJURIES.

ALSO ON THIS DAY, A NEW DEFENSE ATTORNEY, MICHAEL MUSMANO, MAKES ONE FINAL APPEAL TO THE STATE SUPREME JUDICIAL COURT ON THE ISSUE OF JUDGE THAYER'S BIAS.

IT IS DENIED THREE DAYS LATER.

AS THE DATE OF EXECUTION APPROACHES, DEMONSTRATIONS CONTINUE WORLDWIDE.

FROM EUROPE THERE ARE REPORTS OF AMERICAN TOURISTS HARASSED AND ABUSED.

JOSEF STALIN AND BENITO MUSSOLINI, IN THEIR RESPECTIVE COUNTRIES, EXPLOIT THE CAUSE FOR THEIR OWN POLITICAL ENDS.

BOMBS EXPLODE IN THE NEW YORK SUBWAY AND IN A CHURCH IN PHILADELPHIA (AGAIN NO INJURIES).

DOZENS OF PROTESTERS ARE ARRESTED ON THE STREETS OF BOSTON.

MONDAY, AUGUST 22 ON THIS NIGHT, HUGE THRONGS ASSEMBLE IN CITIES AROUND THE WORLD.

A CROWD KEEPS VIGIL AROUND THE STATE PRISON.

SACCO SPENDS HIS FINAL HOURS WITH HIS WIFE.

VANZETTI IS VISITED BY HIS SISTER, LUIGIA, WHO HAS TRAVELLED FROM THEIR HOME IN VILLAFALLETTO.

TUESDAY AUGUST 23 JUST AFTER MIDNIGHT THE PROCESS BEGINS. FIRST TO BE EXECUTED IS THEIR WOULD-BE SAVIOR CELESTINO MADIEROS.

THEN SACCO IS BROUGHT FROM HIS CELL. AS HE IS STRAPPED INTO THE CHAIR HE MAKES HIS FAREWELLS.

MINUTES LATER, VANZETTI IS BROUGHT IN. STRANGELY CALM, HE MAKES HIS FINAL STATEMENT.

VIVA L'ANARCHIA! FAREWELL MY WIFE AND CHILD AND ALL MY FRIENDS! FAREWELL MIA MADRE!

I THANK YOU FOR EVERYTHING YOU HAVE DONE FOR ME. I AM INNOCENT OF ALL CRIME NOT ONLY THIS ONE BUT ALL. I AM AN INNOCENT MAN!

AND THE SWITCH IS PULLED.

I WISH TO FORGIVE SOME PEOPLE FOR WHAT THEY ARE DOING TO ME.

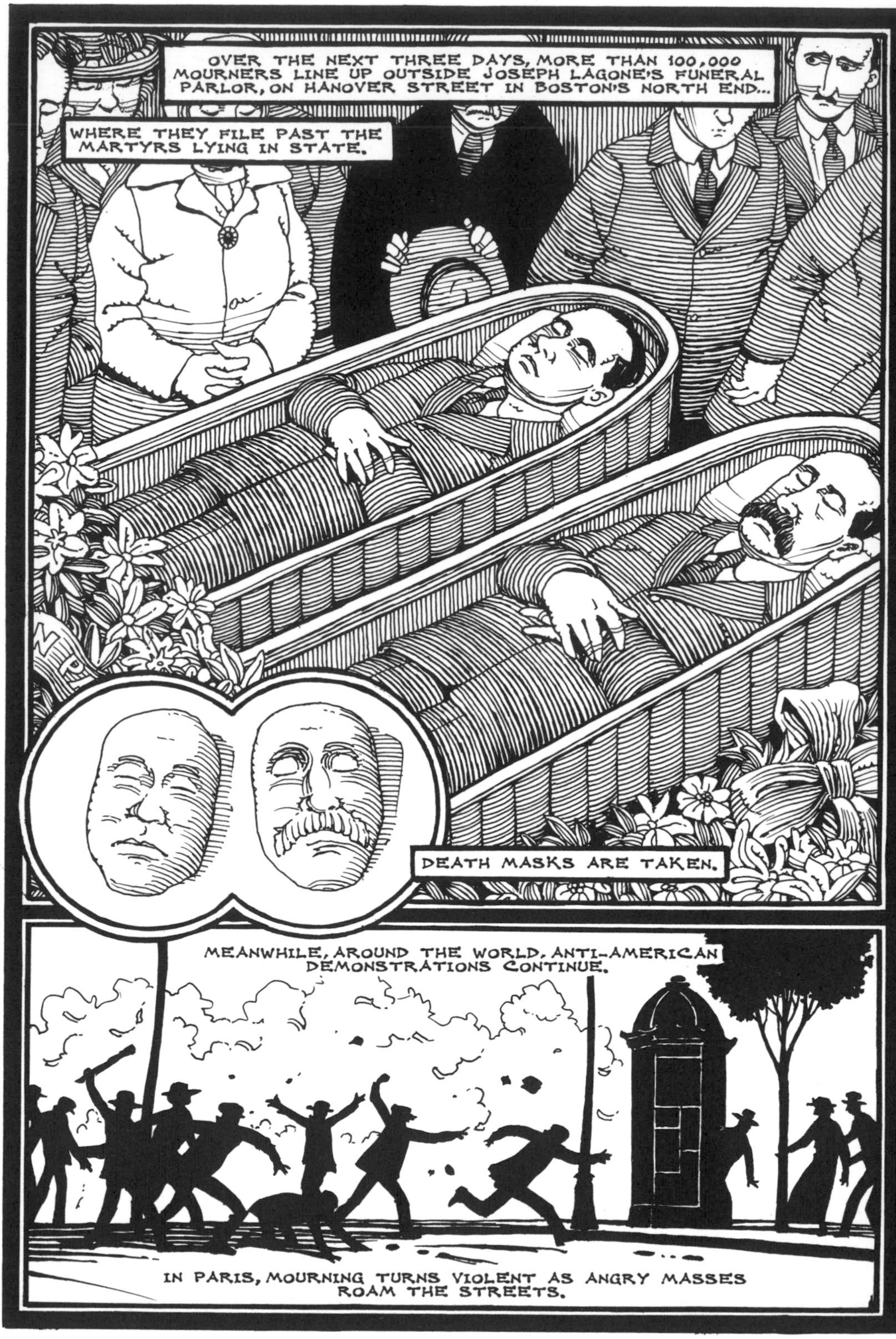
OVER THE NEXT THREE DAYS, MORE THAN 100,000 MOURNERS LINE UP OUTSIDE JOSEPH LAGONE'S FUNERAL PARLOR, ON HANOVER STREET IN BOSTON'S NORTH END...
WHERE THEY FILE PAST THE MARTYRS LYING IN STATE.
DEATH MASKS ARE TAKEN.
MEANWHILE, AROUND THE WORLD, ANTI-AMERICAN DEMONSTRATIONS CONTINUE.
IN PARIS, MOURNING TURNS VIOLENT AS ANGRY MASSES ROAM THE STREETS.

SUNDAY, AUGUST 28
IN A SOAKING RAIN, THE HUGE FUNERAL PROCESSION WINDS ITS WAY THROUGH THE STREETS OF BOSTON. THOUSANDS OF SYMPATHIZERS PARTICIPATE.

MANY WEAR ARMBANDS PROVIDED BY THE DEFENSE COMMITTEE.

REMEMBER **JUSTICE CRUCIFIED** AUGUST 22, 1927

AT ONE POINT THE CROWD IS ATTACKED BY MOUNTED POLICE KEEPING ORDER.

LEAVING MANY BLOODY AND INJURED.

THE PARADE STOPS AT THE GATES OF FOREST HILLS CEMETERY WHERE MARY DONOVAN SAYS A FEW WORDS.

NICOLA SACCO AND BARTOLOMEO VANZETTI YOU CAME TO AMERICA SEEKING FREEDOM. IN YOUR MARTYRDOM WE WILL FIGHT ON AND CONQUER!

THE HEARSES THEN PROCEED TO THE CREMATORIUM.

OVER THE ENSUING YEARS, THE QUESTIONS SURROUNDING THE SACCO-VANZETTI CASE REFUSE TO DIE. WERE THEY ACTUALLY COLD-BLOODED ROBBERS AND MURDERERS? VICTIMS OF A THOROUGHLY CORRUPT SYSTEM? OR PERHAPS BOTH?

FURTHER BALLISTICS TESTS, IN 1961 AND 1983, USING EVER MORE REFINED TECHNOLOGY, CONTINUE TO CONCLUDE THAT THE FATAL BULLET AND SHELL CAME FROM SACCO'S COLT.

BUT THIS DOES NOT SEEM TO SETTLE THINGS.

WHILE CERTAIN OF THEIR EARLIEST SUPPORTERS, SUCH AS CARLO TRESCA, HAVE STATED THEIR BELIEF THAT SACCO, AT LEAST, WAS PROBABLY GUILTY...

OTHERS MAINTAIN THAT THE TESTS REMAIN UNRELIABLE, BECAUSE THE ORIGINAL PISTOL AND AMMUNITION ARE IRRETRIEVABLY TAINTED.

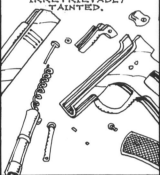

RESOLUTIONS ARE PERIODICALLY INTRODUCED IN THE MASSACHUSETTS LEGISLATURE TO PARDON POSTHUMOUSLY THE TWO MEN.

BUT THEY ARE DEFEATED EVERY TIME.

AT LAST, IN 1977, UPON THE 50TH ANNIVERSARY OF THE EXECUTIONS, GOVERNOR MICHAEL DUKAKIS DECLARES THAT:

ANY STIGMA OR DISGRACE SHOULD FOREVER BE REMOVED FROM THE NAMES OF NICOLA SACCO AND BARTOLOMEO VANZETTI.

A MEMORIAL PLAQUE, DESIGNED BY THE FAMED SCULPTOR GUTZON BORGLUM, IS FINALLY ACCEPTED BY THE COMMONWEALTH IN 1997.

WHAT I WISH MORE THAN A LAST HOUR OF AGONY IS CASE AND OUR FATE MAY BE UND IN THEIR REAL BEING AN AS A TREMENDOUS L THE FORCES OF F SO THAT OUR SUFFERING AND WILL NOT HAVE BEEN IN V

IS IS NOW ON DISPLAY IN THE BOSTON PIUBLIC LIBRARY.

EVEN TODAY, WITH THE ISSUES OF THEIR TIME LARGELY FORGOTTEN, CONTROVERSY SURROUNDING THE LIVES OF SACCO AND VANZETTI REFUSES TO ABATE.

THEY ARE GUILTY:

BULLET III CONTINUES TO IMPLICATE SACCO. IF THE BULLETS WERE SWITCHED HOW WAS IT KEPT A SECRET FOR SO LONG?

THE VARIETY OF BULLETS FOUND IN SACCO'S POSSESSION MATCHED THOSE FROM THE CRIME SCENE.

THE OBSOLETE TYPE OF WINCHESTER BULLETS CARRIED BY SACCO ALSO MATCHED THOSE USED IN THE CRIME.

IF SACCO IS GUILTY THE WITNESSES ARE MOST LIKELY CORRECT IN THEIR IDENTIFICATIONS OF BOTH MEN.

WHY WERE THE MEN SO HEAVILY ARMED ON THE NIGHT OF THEIR ARREST?

IF THEY WERE OUT TO WARN THEIR FRIENDS ABOUT IMPENDING RAIDS, WHY DID THEY WAIT FIVE DAYS BEFORE FIRST BECOMING CONCERNED?

WHY DID THEY NOT HIDE THEIR OWN RADICAL LITERATURE?

THE POLITICAL BELIEFS OF BOTH MEN WOULD TEND TO JUSTIFY ROBBERY AND MURDER AS ANOTHER BATTLE IN THE ONGOING CLASS WAR.

THEY ARE INNOCENT:

THE WHEREABOUTS OF BOTH MEN ON THE DAY OF THE CRIME WAS ATTESTED TO BY UNSHAKABLE WITNESSES.

EYEWITNESSES AT THE SCENE RECALLED THAT THE BANDITS SPOKE WITH NO ACCENTS.

THE $15776. 51 IN STOLEN PAYROL CASH WAS NEVER TRACED OR RECOVERED.

THE OTHER BANDITS IN THE GANG WERE NEVER IDENTIFIED.

WHY IS BULLET III DIFFERENT? DIDN'T THE CORONER CONCLUDE THAT ALL SIX BULLETS CAME FROM THE SAME GUN?

AFTER THE CRIME, BOTH MEN CONTINUED TO GO ABOUT THEIR LIVES: NO ATTEMPT TO FLEE OR TO ALTER THEIR FAMILIAR PATTERNS.

IF THE CRIME WAS COMMITTED IN THE NAME OF THEIR CAUSE, WHY DID THEY NOT CLAIM CREDIT FOR IT INSTEAD OF REPEATEDLY AND EMPHATICALLY ASSERTING THEIR INNOCENCE?

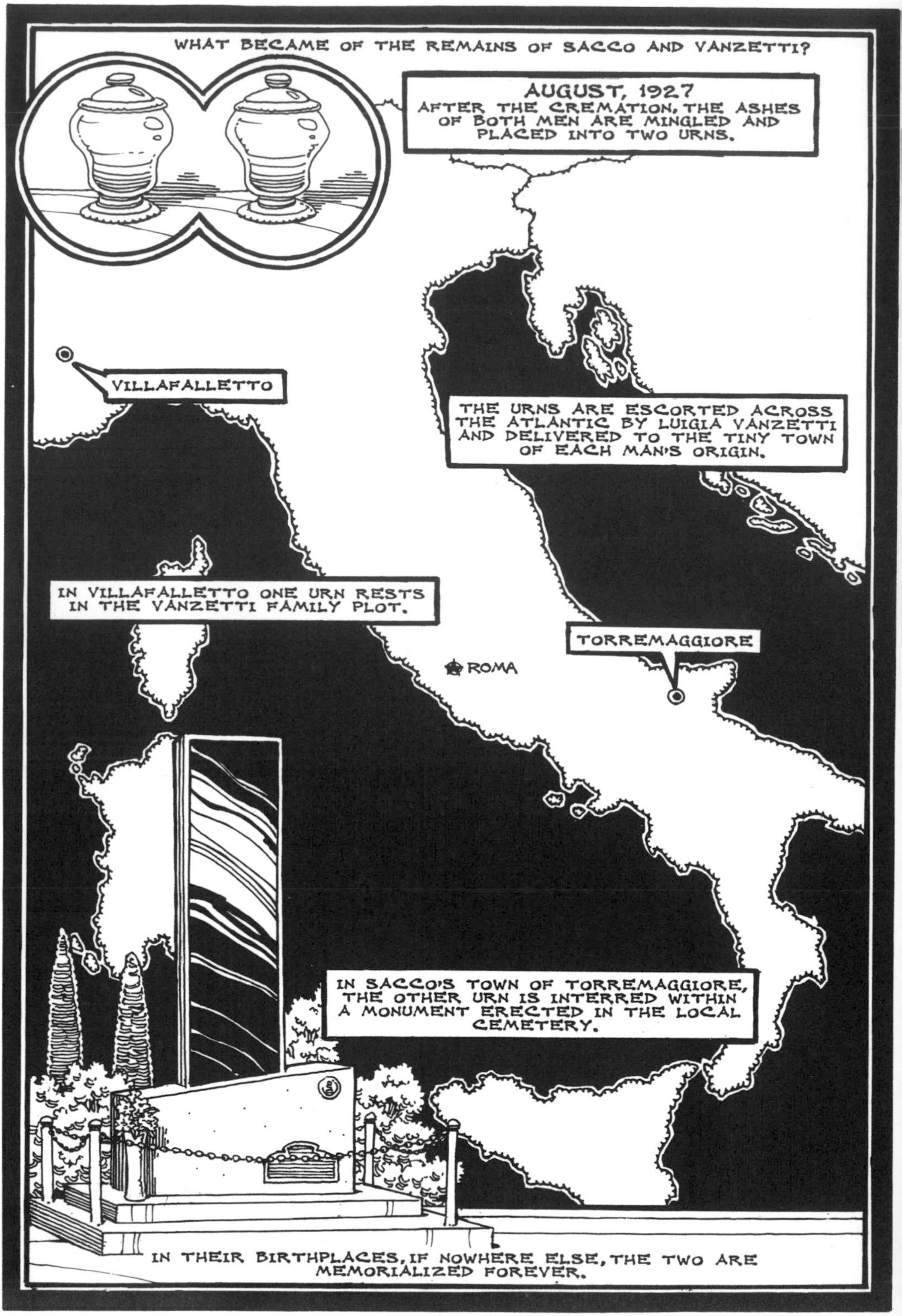
WHAT BECAME OF THE REMAINS OF SACCO AND VANZETTI?
AUGUST, 1927
AFTER THE CREMATION, THE ASHES OF BOTH MEN ARE MINGLED AND PLACED INTO TWO URNS.
VILLAFALLETTO
THE URNS ARE ESCORTED ACROSS THE ATLANTIC BY LUIGIA VANZETTI AND DELIVERED TO THE TINY TOWN OF EACH MAN'S ORIGIN.
IN VILLAFALLETTO ONE URN RESTS IN THE VANZETTI FAMILY PLOT.
TORREMAGGIORE
ROMA
IN SACCO'S TOWN OF TORREMAGGIORE, THE OTHER URN IS INTERRED WITHIN A MONUMENT ERECTED IN THE LOCAL CEMETERY.
IN THEIR BIRTHPLACES, IF NOWHERE ELSE, THE TWO ARE MEMORIALIZED FOREVER.